PATCHWORK
PERSUASION

Fascinating Quilts from Traditional Designs

Joen Wolfrom

C&T PUBLISHING

©1997 Joen Wolfrom

Cover: *Sunlight and Winds* by Junko Sawada, Yokohama-shi, Japan

Editor: Liz Aneloski
Copy Editor: Judith M. Moretz, Pleasant Hill, California
Technical Editor: Joyce Engels Lytle
Design Director: Diane Pedersen
Book Designer: Riba Taylor, Sebastopol, California
Cover Designers: Kathy Lee and John Cram
Computer Illustrators: Joen Wolfrom and Kandy Petersen
(Illustrations were produced using Macromedia Freehand 5.0 Software.)
Photographer: Ken Wagner, Wagner Photo Lab, Seattle, Washington
(unless otherwise noted)

Published by C&T Publishing, P.O. Box 1456, Lafayette, California 94549

Library of Congress Cataloging-in-Publication Data

Wolfrom, Joen.
    Patchwork persuasion : fascinating quilts from traditional designs
  / Joen Wolfrom.
        p.   cm.
    Includes bibliographical references and index.
    ISBN 1-57120-027-4
    1. Patchwork quilts—Design.   2. Patchwork.   I. Title.
TT835.W64423   1997
746.46'041—dc21   96-29559
                                                              CIP

Printed in China

10 9 8 7 6 5 4 3 2

Contents

* Photo numbers match the page numbers on which they appear.

Acknowledgments

So many tasks are involved when a book is written. Much is done behind the scenes by people who work long hours doing laborious chores which take extreme concentration and accuracy. I wish to thank all who had major roles to play in bringing this book to fruition.

I so enjoyed working with Liz Aneloski, my diligent, kind, organized, and empathetic editor. Her gentle guidance was wonderful, and her suggestions well suited. I enjoyed our experience together immensely. Additionally, it was a special treat to have an editor who is also a mother of active children. She could relate to the dilemma of an author fitting deadlines into a hectic, sometimes out-of-control, schedule and life.

Joyce Lytle, technical editor, is a master at detail work. She does an extraordinary job making certain all is in order. In my earliest books this job was left to the editor and author. It was an enormous, time-consuming task to do well. Having done it previously, I can be very appreciative of all that Joyce accomplishes. In addition, she is always upbeat and gracious. It was delightful working with Joyce on yet another book.

Judith Moretz, my wonderful copy editor, watches over my writing to make certain my words are not only correct, but understandable. I admire Judy's superb ability to handle the English language to perfection. It's difficult to see one's own writing clearly when composing a book. Having taught both English grammar and creative writing in my past teaching career, naturally I would prefer my own writing to be clear and accurate. Thus, I am fortunate to have Judith oversee my writing and make necessary changes.

Although I wanted to create my own illustrations for this book, I could not pretend to be *the illustrator*. I needed a professional illustrator who was willing to take my designs and ideas and make them perfect. Kandy Petersen took on this task with exuberance. I so appreciate the fact that Kandy was willing to work with my illustrations in all their varied colorations, and she did so in a delightfully positive manner. Kandy's generous effort made a tremendous difference in the visual outcome of *Patchwork Persuasion*. I am so pleased we were able to combine our creative efforts.

Ken Wagner is one of the leading quilt and textile art photographers in our country. Photographing quilts well is a difficult task, even for professional photographers. Ken's knowledge and skill in capturing color, design, and quilting lines on fabric is extraordinary. I am extremely pleased to have been able to use Ken's photographic talents whenever possible. His care, patience, personality, calm manner, and efficiency were appreciated greatly.

Other important players in this book-making task were Riba Taylor, book designer, and Kathy Lee and John Cram, book cover designers. Designing a book so that it is inviting to the reader is an unusual talent. I thank Riba for her organizational skills, talent, and professional ability to bring manuscript, photos, and illustrations together into a visually successful book. Thanks also to Kathy and John for bringing together their creative abilities to design an appropriate book cover.

I wish to give a special thanks to my friends and colleagues who have so willingly shared their own creative expressions and wonderful talents. This book's visual success is due to your beautiful and exciting contributions. I am spellbound by your many amazing feats and talents. I thank you for your most generous spirit. May you have many years of stimulating creativity. It is my pleasure to include your work. Thanks so very much: Deirdre Amsden, Ellen Anderson, Sue Atlas, Joy Baaklini, Marcia Baker, Debra Baum, Emilie Belak, Judy Breytenbach, Karen Combs, Kathy Cosgrove, Helen Courtice, Lorraine DeLaO, Sarah Dickson, Philomena Durcan, Joan Dyer, Diane Ebner, Sylvia Einstein, Cynthia England, Caryl Bryer Fallert, Beth Gilbert, Linda Gill, Mary Gillis, Barbara Godfrey, Jane Hall, Gloria Hansen, Laura Heine, Sharla Hicks, Peggy Hill, Judy House, Wendy Hrabowsky, Rosey Hunt, Martie Huston, Jane Kakaley, Lynda Kelley, Shirley Kelly, Anita Krug, Nobuko Kubota, Sylvia Kundrats, The Ladies of the Lake of Manitowoc County, Wisconsin, Kay Lettau, Jean Liittschwager, Jack and Harriet MacDuff, Marion Marias, Grania McElligott, Maureen McGee, Margaret Miller, Erika Odemer, Reynola Pakusich, Jennie Peck, Katherine Picot, Christine Porter, Kaye Rhodes, Janice Richards, Wendy Richardson, Junko Sawada, Donna Schneider, Margaret Schucker, Paul Schutte, Arlene Stamper, Dorle Stern-Straeter, Connie Tenpas, The Tuesday Quilters and Friends, Lynn Underwood, Kathy Vitek, Diana Voyer, Carol Webb, Judy White, Sue Williams, Jane Willoughby Scott, and Lucy Zeldenrust.

Finally, I wish to thank conference sponsors, organization members, educational faculties, and editors who have invited me to teach, lecture, write, and share my ideas and knowledge. I am filled with gratitude for all of you who have participated in these activities over the years. I am overwhelmed by your wonderful support, encouragement, and friendship. It is because of you, and for you, that this book has been written.

Fondly,

Joen

I dedicate this book

To
Lenni Markovich,
a friend and instructor who brings joy into my life.
Lenni has so generously put balance into my life
by providing me with daily opportunities
to stretch my muscles, unclog my brain,
and feel mentally and physically energized.
May we both live to reap the best that life offers.

To
my father, Winslow Barger
who has had to face extraordinary challenges
and take on new roles
in his eighth decade of life.
He has given all who know him
even more reasons to admire his courage,
positive attitude, and tenacity.
May his life continue to be filled with
love, joy, curiosity, and golf!

To
Louise Townsend,
a special friend and wonderful editor
who will always be cherished.
Her sweet, caring manner, humor,
and contagious laughter
will be remembered
forever.

Foreword

I am excited to present to you *Patchwork Persuasion,* a book that has been waiting in the wings for a very long time! It has been on my "to write" list for C&T since 1991.

The ideas for *Patchwork Persuasion* began in the late 1970s. It was then I began paying closer attention to the block patterns I chose for my quilts. Whenever I became disappointed in my results, I tried to assess the reasons for my dissatisfaction. I found there was an art to block selection and eventually I gained enough courage and experience to make other determinations about block interaction and overall settings. Hence, my innovative block exploration commenced.

I found there were innumerable ways to enhance block designs: some pattern lines may be added while others can be eliminated. Blocks or block sections may be rotated for greater design flexibility. New designs can be created through block merges or block explosions. Fascinating illusions can be made by stretching or condensing blocks or parts of blocks. Even making color and value changes can bring spectacular results through illusionary play. Value play can lead to de-emphasizing block parts. A great effect can be created by moving one block's pattern into another block's boundaries. Even further block play led me to find new ways to promote greater flexibility. These ideas included dropping rows of blocks, varying the block sizes, floating blocks above the background, and staggering the blocks throughout the surface.

Soon I had more ideas, drawings, and in-progress projects than I could manage. Sharing these concepts in a class seemed like a great idea. So in 1984 I began organizing my ideas and writing my first of many lesson plans for this class. Thus the workshop Stretching Traditions was born, and ready to be offered in 1985 to anyone who was interested. At first most workshop sponsors were apprehensive about offering such a class,

as the ideas seemed too radical. By the early 1990s there was a swing in attitude, and many quilters were eager to incorporate new ideas into their quilts. So the workshop Stretching Traditions began gaining in popularity. Currently it is one of the most requested workshops I offer.

Patchwork Persuasion is based on the concepts I teach in my workshop Stretching Traditions. It has been my goal to make *Patchwork Persuasion* a reader-friendly book with a multitude of ideas, supported by well-sequenced, colorful illustrations. I am exceptionally excited to offer this book as a resource companion to all quilters who are looking for ways to create unique quilts based on traditional block patterns. I hope quilting teachers will be excited to create classes based on this book's concepts, and also will use *Patchwork Persuasion* as a student resource for current classes.

As in *The Visual Dance,* I must confess to having written too much material for my allotted 144 pages. Therefore six chapters have had to be eliminated. These orphaned chapters will be the foundation of a sequel— undoubtedly my next writing project.

I hope the concepts in *Patchwork Persuasion* excite and energize you into creating fascinating quilts. Read, enjoy, and create!

A Gallery of Creative Inspiration

7A. *Reef*, 1994, 75½" x 48"
Judy Breytenbach, Kloof, South Africa

This breathtaking quilt vibrates with
dynamic colors. Judy's inspiration to
make *Reef* came from Marcia Karlin's
(Lincolnshire, Illinois) quilt, which she
had seen in the September, 1991, issue of
Quilting International. Photo: Malcolm
Funston, Kloof, South Africa

7B. *Ruel's Kaleidoscope,* 1991, 43" x 63"
Sharla Hicks, Anaheim, California

Using the Kaleidoscope block, Sharla designed her quilt using the
block's individual shapes rather than making units of blocks. She
designed her quilt on a wall, moving pieces and small units until
visual balance was achieved. Photo: Courtesy of the artist

8A. *Utopia,* 1995, 83" x 83"
Nobuko Kubota, Tokyo, Japan

Utopia was created to express the beautiful relationship between Nobuko and her friends. She used the Star Wonder and Hanis Point patterns to create her original design. Her star of the April-born is Taurus. Here Taurus, a constellation in the Northern Hemisphere, is shown spreading into the Milky Way (*Amano-Gawa*). The middle star represents Nobuko while her friends' stars surround and support her. The six stars combine to form "The Bull." The star colors for Nobuko's friends have been chosen to match their personalities. Photo: Courtesy of the artist

8B. *Utopia,* 1995, detail
Nobuko Kubota, Tokyo, Japan

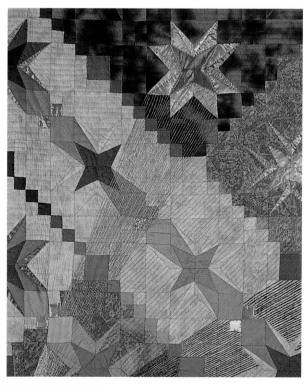

8C. *Utopia,* 1995, detail
Nobuko Kubota, Tokyo, Japan

9A. *Sunlight and Winds*, 1994, 74½" x 85½"
Junko Sawada, Yokohama-Shi, Japan

Junko began creating her design for this beautiful quilt with the
traditional blocks Basket and Lily. Her innovative style allows the
quilt to reflect the free spirit of the garden, as she provides
movement of leaves and flowers. The quilt was inspired by the
scene of Kensington Palace garden in London and the memory of a
William Morris design. Photo: Sharon Risedorph

10A. *Bird's Song*, 1995, 68" x 79"
Junko Sawada, Yokohama-Shi, Japan

Junko has given the traditional Lily pattern a contemporary composition and coloration. Her beautiful manner of color placement brings forth a lovely, subtle design with birds flying in the distance. Photo: Courtesy of the artist

10B. *View from My Childhood Garden,* 1988, 64" x 84"
Joen Wolfrom, Fox Island, Washington

The impressionistic strip-pieced landscape was commissioned by the Ulster Folk and Transport Museum in Northern Ireland. They requested a design which reflected the author's homeland in America's beautiful Pacific Northwest. Joen created a scene overlooking Puget Sound and the Olympic Mountains during the spring time blooming of rhododendrons and azaleas. Photo: Ken Wagner

11A. *Koinonia Garden*, 1988, 62" x 94"
Arlene Stamper, San Diego, California

This beautiful lily friendship quilt was inspired by a quilt made by Ruth McDonnell which Arlene had seen at the 1983 Quilters' Guild of England exhibit. Once home, Arlene drafted a lily pattern and proceeded to design her own quilt. Arlene has created a very popular masterpiece, as this quilt has been duplicated by many quiltmakers throughout the world—sometimes with exact color and fabric placement. If you see other quilts done similarly, note this is the original quilt, which has inspired so many renditions.

Friendship Lily blocks were made by Jan Moffatt, Connie St. Michel, Margie Potter, Harriet Love, Mary Lou Barkham, Nancy Nichols, Arlene Stamper, Janie Schott, Sharyn Craig, Joan Stuart, Kathleen Hogan, Louise Hixon, Peggie Hunter, Diana Lentz, Anne Michener, Sue Chapel, Mary Jo Manzur, Eleanor Steddom, Regina Spurgeon, Patty Smith, Debby Timby, and Georgie Bjornson. Arlene sewed the blocks together, made the innovative border, and hand quilted the quilt. Photo: Carina Woolrich; Courtesy of Quilt San Diego

12A. *Awakenings*, 1992, 66" x 66"
Gloria Hansen, Hightstown, New Jersey

Gloria's original design is based on a
repeat block she drew on graph paper.
Gloria arranged the design so that the
concentration of color occurred in the
center and then extended outward.
Photo: Courtesy of the artist

12B. *Sometimes You Just Have to Work Through the Blues*, 1994, 90" x 90"
Margaret Schucker, Rancho Palos Verdes, California

Margaret began with the traditional block pattern Kansas Trouble.
Her blue value changes, moving from light in the center to dark at
the edges, create a wonderful illusion of luster. Luster is then
accentuated in the border. The result is a show-stopping innovative
traditional quilt. Photo: Courtesy of Leman Publications

13A. *Celtic Clan,* 1991, 52" x 52"
Philomena Durcan, Sunnyvale, California

Philomena has created a lovely sampler quilt using her own Celtic designs. *Celtic Clan* is a wonderful example of a visually successful sampler quilt. Unity, harmony, and visual balance are all present. (To order books by Philomena, see Sources.)
Photo: Courtesy of the artist

13B. *Fractured Rings,* 1991, 68" x 78"
Grania McElligott, Naas, Ireland

Grania has created a contemporary quilt using the traditional Double Wedding Ring pattern. She has used a beautiful blend of silk fabrics. By spontaneous color placement and value changes, Grania has created an exquisite quilt illustrating the succesful merging of contemporary design with traditional roots. Photo: Tony Hurst

13C. *She's All at Sea,* 1994, 42" x 56"
Rosey Hunt, Las Vegas, Nevada

Rosey created *She's All at Sea* as a tribute to her daughter's service in the British Royal Navy. Rosey has used the block Storm at Sea to represent the continuous waves which surround the imagery. Varying the block sizes allowed Rosey to increase the visual interest. She used dozens of different fabrics to create the Storm at Sea waves. This resulted in wonderful sea movement, transparency, and a woven ribbon effect through-out the border. Photo: Courtesy of the artist

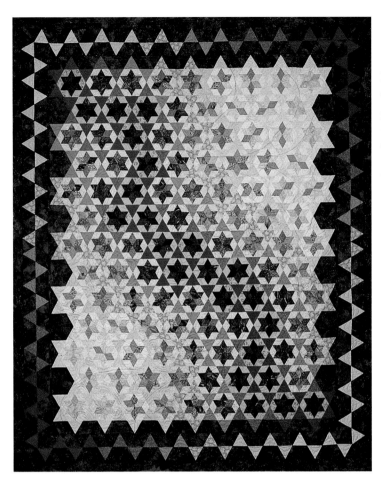

14A. *Galaxy of Stars,* 1996, 82" x 98"
Marcia Baker, Plano, Texas

This innovatively-colored six-pointed star quilt was strip-pieced using Marcia's own technique (See Sources). Her colorful quilt was inspired by a set of Tupperware cups sitting on her kitchen counter. It took her a year to collect the wide variety of fabrics she used to create her own star galaxy. Photo: Orland Baker

14B. *Bethany Beach,* 1995, 39" x 66"
Beth Gilbert, Buffalo Grove, Illinois

This memory quilt is a warm reminder of a Bethany Beach family vacation. Using the Snail's Trail pattern as her foundation, Beth incorporated umbrella, children (niece and nephew), and pails into the Snail's Trail base. Quilting was created to follow the sun's rays. The "beach" border includes shells, sequins, and beads. The Snail's Trail pattern was paper-pieced. Photo: Courtesy of the artist

15A. *Canada Geese Metamorphosis*, 1991, 88" x 108"
Emilie Belak, Grand Forks, British Columbia, Canada

The triangles of the Flying Geese pattern are arranged as mountains of British Columbia. Emilie arranged these so the darkest triangles were at the bottom while the lightest ones were toward the top, representing mist in fall. For more details about this quilt, see page 127. Photo: Courtesy of the artist

15B. *Chroma IV: Canyon*, 1994, 44" x 44"
Jane Hall, Raleigh, North Carolina

Jane has created a unique colorwash quilt using the Pineapple Log Cabin block. Because of her subtle color use, the individual blocks have been masked. She used hand-dyed sueded cotton fabric, and added one-half inch window panes to frame the blocks. Photo: Ken Wagner

15C. *The Last Panda*, 1995, 19" x 35"
Shirley Kelly, Colden, New York

This quilt was inspired by an acrylic painting by Lee Kromschroeder and Shirley's desire to use this author's landscape strip-piecing technique. Having fallen in love with this particular painting, Shirley decided to make her own rendition of the scene. The bamboo leaves are hand appliquéd. Photo: Ken Wagner

16A. *Transition*, 1992, 70" x 45"
Jean Liittschwager, Leaburg, Oregon

This quilt was designed to pay tribute to both the beauty of the forest and the transition of time in life, which is represented by the joyful dawn and the peaceful dusk. This was a commission created for the Celeste Campbell Senior Center in Eugene, Oregon. Photo: Jean Liittschwager

16B. *Starlit Night*, 1984, 75" x 87"
Dorle Stern-Straeter, München, Germany

Starlit Night has been created by combining two blocks: one has straight lines; the other has curved lines. Their interaction creates wonderful movement throughout the quilt. Cotton and silk fabrics blend beautifully to create the imagery. Photo: Wolfgang Zuppée

16C. *Leaves*, 1995, 18" x 40"
Wendy Hrabowsky, Chester, Nova Scotia, Canada

Being an extremely innovative quilter, Wendy sewed together only the leaf portions of the traditional Maple Leaf pattern. Then she appliquéd her maple leaves onto background fabric. She then stitched these two layers onto a foundation at the edge of the leaves. Wendy quilted swirling curved lines throughout the design to represent the wind blowing the leaves to the ground. Photo: Courtesy of the artist

Setting the Stage

Beginning the Journey

When I began quilting in the early 1970s, I was in awe of all traditional designs, and saw each of them through rose-colored glasses. I envisioned spending scores of years happily creating dozens of traditional quilts. I carefully duplicated each pattern I used. I never dreamt of changing any part of a traditional block pattern.

About seven years into my quiltmaking hobby, I was excited about beginning a new quilt. I loved the block pattern and the fabrics I had chosen. I could hardly wait to put scissors to cloth. Before proceeding, however, I made a small paper-block quilt to give me an idea as to how the block's pattern would fit together in a quilt format. To my surprise, I found the overall pattern disappointing. After pondering my dilemma, I realized I could take one of three courses: make the quilt as planned; find another pattern; or change the pattern to strengthen its design. With considerable guilt and tentativeness, I chose the latter path. I added lines, which created new shapes, thereby giving the design more substance.

From then on, I couldn't make a traditional quilt without changing the pattern in some way. As time went on, I became intrigued with the limitless types of changes that could be made. As I experimented, I found my ideas stretched farther than my time. Frustratingly, I could only create a small portion of the quilts that were in my head. It became obvious I could never play with all the design ideas that danced in my mind.

Lack of time continues to plague me, as it does most of us. Since many of these ideas have been bubbling in my mind for almost two decades, and my scraps of paper and design ideas are spilling out of drawers and cupboards uncontrollably, it is past time to share with you what I have been attempting or yearning to do. Perhaps this compilation of concepts will give you incentive to play with these ideas or explore further on your own. I find the possibilities fascinating. In recent years I have noticed other quiltmakers experimenting and thinking along some of the same lines as I. It is fun to see such innovation in our field. I hope you find many wonderful traditional surprises in this book to tickle your fancy. But before beginning our fun-filled exploration, we should review a few vital design points.

Creating a Well-Designed Quilt

A traditional design can be balanced through color choices, fabric use, or appropriate block placement within the total design setting. The latter can be achieved easily. Here are a few suggestions to make certain you will gain the greatest potential from your selected pattern.

THE HORIZONTAL "UNEVEN" RULE

Generally, most quilt designs look better when the number of blocks in a horizontal row is uneven, such as three, five, seven, or nine blocks. Since we automatically focus on the horizontal center of the quilt, our eyes are drawn to the middle block design, as in Illusionary Star (Figure 1-1). When there is an even number of blocks horizontally, our eyes still focus on the center of the quilt, which is usually only background. In fact, we have to force our eyes to look away from the center to the quilt's overall design. This happens often with a four-block quilt. Notice how your eyes move right to the center background in Figure 1-2. You have to force your eyes outward to stay focused on the intended design—the stars.

There are exceptions to this uneven horizontal block rule. A few traditional patterns need an even number of horizontal blocks to create a balanced design. One such example is the Log Cabin Barn Raising (Figure 1-3).

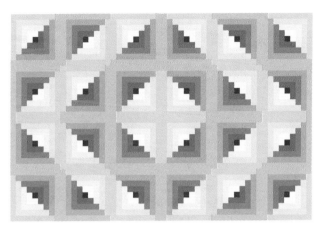

FIGURE 1-3

Occasionally a traditional pattern needs an even number of horizontal blocks to create a balanced design. One such example of this exception is the Log Cabin Barn-Raising design.

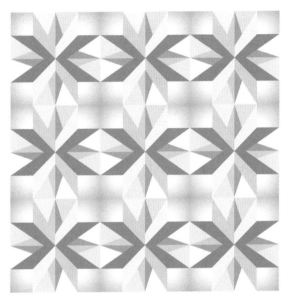

FIGURE 1-1

As a rule, an uneven number of horizontal blocks in a setting is a better choice than an even number, because the former creates a mid-point focus of the featured block's main attraction—it's foreground design. Here our eyes focus on the center star with three horizontal blocks used. (Illusionary Star © Joen Wolfrom 1996)

Surprisingly, block patterns can create unexpected new designs when they are put together in an even-block setting. Through the Looking Glass does this (Figures 1-4A and B). In Figure 1-4B, its four-block setting focuses on an interesting circular design with a violet square center. This pattern, then, can be used quite successfully with only four blocks. Occasionally a horizontally-even block design can turn out to be as good as, or even more interesting than, the uneven setting. Unfortunately, it is almost impossible to predict how a multi-block pattern will look when you see only one block.

FIGURE 1-2

Most four-block settings create an accidental focus on the design center's background. When this happens, we have to force our eyes to look at the outer stars, as shown in this example of Illusionary Star.

FIGURE 1-4A

Through the Looking Glass (seven-patch pattern: 14 x 14 = 195 square grid) (© Joen Wolfrom 1994)

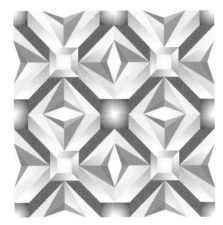

FIGURE 1-4B

An interesting center design can appear unexpectedly in a four-block setting in some patterns. This happens in the pattern Through the Looking Glass.

Some block patterns have no particular reaction to their horizontal setting. They can be placed in either an even or uneven horizontal block setting. The Log Cabin Straight Furrows pattern is such an example (Figure 1-5).

FIGURE 1-5

A few traditional patterns have no particular reaction to their setting. They can be placed in either an even or uneven horizontal block setting with success. The Log Cabin Straight Furrows pattern is such an example.

Because it is difficult to visualize how blocks will interact, it is a good idea to make a paper quilt of your pattern, so you are not working blindly with the design. Usually this can be done with two-inch paper blocks. If the block's design is complicated, use three- or four-inch paper blocks. Find the best arrangement for your blocks; choose to display them to their best advantage. This will eliminate unfortunate surprises when your quilt top is put together.

FITTING THE BLOCK DESIGN TO THE BED

To help determine how many blocks will fit across your bed, see the mattress chart below. Decide how many blocks will fit best across the top of your bed. Then divide the mattress width by the number of blocks to determine the block size. You can adjust the size of the block to fit this measurement. After you determine the size and number of blocks needed to cover the bed top, decide how many blocks and what size border you want to extend down the bed sides. Once your plans are finalized, draft the pattern to exact specifications.

Type of Mattress	Mattress Width x Length
crib, six-year	27" x 52"
twin, regular	39" x 75"
twin, long	39" x 80"
double, regular	54" x 75"
double, long	54" x 80"
queen	60" x 80"
king, regular	76" x 80"
king, California	72" x 84"
king, dual	78" x 80"
king, water bed	72" x 84"

Anatomy of a Quilt Block

Understanding the anatomy of a quilt block will ease your work at almost every level of quiltmaking. Knowing how blocks are made gives you the freedom to be innovative. If you understand how a block pattern is designed, you will gain flexibility by being able to move blocks within the design, change the inside parts of blocks, create exciting new designs, and increase your blocks' background options. Many possibilities will be presented in later chapters.

As you may be aware, every block family (four-patch, nine-patch, five-patch, seven-patch, eight-pointed star, etc.) has its own anatomy or skeletal system from which each pattern is made. A block's skeleton is a layer of lines from which to draw the actual block pattern. This layer of lines works like custom-made graph paper.

Each *patch-pattern family* has its own personal graph paper, which is not interchangeable with another patch pattern family's set of lines. Eight-pointed star patterns and designs based on circles use a different type of graphing than the patch-patterns. Their custom-made layers of lines are not based on gridded squares, but on uniquely placed lines, which relate only to each family of patterns. Regardless of the traditional pattern you choose, it will fit only into one family's skeletal system. When working with two or more block patterns, choose blocks that are members of the same family, because they have a compatible makeup, or the same family roots.

FAMILY ROOTS

If you are working with nine-patch patterns, most blocks will be broken into three or six equal parts, horizontally and vertically (Figures 1-6 and 1-7). The lines forming these divisions are the *grid lines*. Every nine-patch pattern uses these grid lines and their intersecting points to create its design. Shoofly and Card Tricks are members of this pattern family (Figures 1-8 and 1-9). When two nine-patch designs are placed side by side, the pattern pieces fit together, because they have identical grid lines (Figures 1-10). If well matched, block patterns from the same family create a harmonious design together (Figure 1-11).

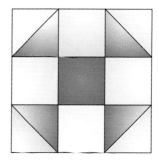

FIGURE 1-8

Shoofly (nine-patch pattern: 3 x 3 = 9 square grid)

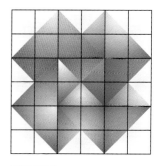

FIGURE 1-9

Card Tricks (nine-patch pattern: 3 x 3 = 9 and 6 x 6 = 36 square grid)

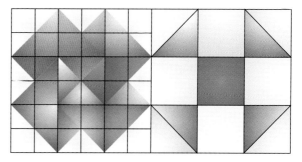

FIGURE 1-10

With identical grid lines, different nine-patch patterns fit well together. Card Tricks and Shoofly are good partners because they belong to the same grid family.

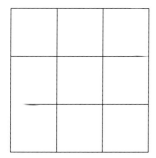

FIGURE 1-6

A nine-patch block is divided into three equal divisions horizontally and vertically. This results in the block being divided into nine small grid squares, which are used as reference points when the pattern is drafted.

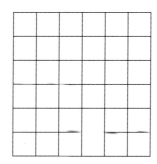

FIGURE 1-7

If a nine-patch block is divided again, there will be six horizontal and vertical divisions resulting in 36 squares (6 x 6 = 36 square grid). Many nine-patch patterns need this additional gridding for pattern drafting.

FIGURE 1-11

Shoofly and Card Tricks create a successful union with their nine-patch family relationship.

When working with four-patch patterns, again, the pattern development is based on the grid lines and their intersecting points. A basic four-patch pattern is divided into two equal divisions, horizontally and vertically. The result is four equal squares in the block (Figure 1-12). Most often the block is divided in four or eight equal divisions (Figures 1-13A and B). You can create numerous patterns by using these grid markings to draw a block pattern's lines. Two four-patch patterns are Road to Oklahoma and Double X, No. 3 (Figures 1-14 and 1-15). When two four-patch patterns are placed together, their grid lines meet and the individual pattern pieces fit together comfortably (Figure 1-16A and B).

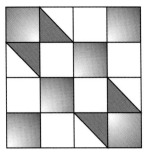

FIGURE 1-14

Road to Oklahoma (four-patch pattern: 4 x 4 = 16 square grid)

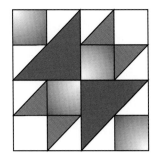

FIGURE 1-15

Double X, No. 3 (four-patch pattern: 4 x 4 = 16 square grid)

FIGURE 1-16A

Road to Oklahoma and the Double X, No. 3 fit together because they are both from the four-patch pattern family.

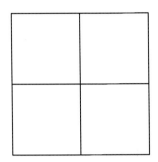

FIGURE 1-12

A simple four-patch pattern is divided into two equal parts horizontally and vertically. This results in four equal sections (2 x 2 = 4 square grid).

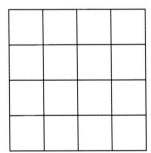

FIGURE 1-13A

Many four-patch block patterns are divided into four equal divisions horizontally and vertically. This results in the block being divided into sixteen small grid squares (4 x 4 = 16 square grid). These are used as reference points when a pattern is drafted.

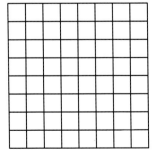

FIGURE 1-13B

Some four-patch patterns need to be broken into eight equal divisions horizontally and vertically to create their design grids. When this is done, the block is divided into sixty-four small squares (8 x 8 = 64 square grid).

FIGURE 1-16B

Road to Oklahoma and the Double X, No. 3 work together to create a new design in a twenty-five block setting.

Like the nine- and four-patch families, the five-patch family uses grid lines and reference points to create its designs. Usually these are divided into five or ten equal divisions, horizontally and vertically (Figures 1-17 and 1-18). Any design which evolves from this gridded skeleton is considered a five-patch pattern. Two examples are Hope of Hartford and Tulip Time (Figures 1-19 and 1-20). Two five-patch patterns fit together well because of their common elements (Figures 1-21 and 1-22).

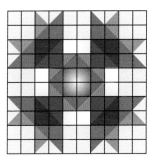

FIGURE 1-20

Tulip Time (five-patch pattern: 10 x 10 = 100 square grid) (© Joen Wolfrom 1996)

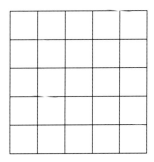

FIGURE 1-17

A five-patch block is divided into five equal parts horizontally and vertically. This results in the block being divided into twenty-five small grid squares, which are used as reference points when the pattern is drafted (5 x 5 = 25 square grid).

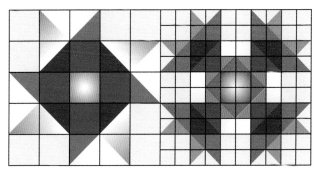

FIGURE 1-21

Hope of Hartford and Tulip Time work well together because both are members of the five-patch pattern family.

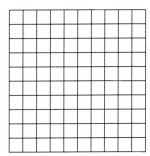

FIGURE 1-18

A complex five-patch pattern may need to be divided further. When this is done, there will be ten horizontal and vertical divisions (10 x 10 = 100 square grid).

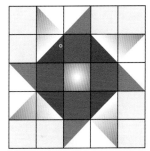

FIGURE 1-19

Hope of Hartford (five-patch pattern: 5 x 5 = 25 square grid)

FIGURE 1-22

The five-patch pattern combination of Hope of Hartford and Tulip Time show good patch-pattern family unity.

The seven-patch family uses a gridding system that divides each block into seven or fourteen equal parts (Figures 1-23 and 1-24). From this gridding system you can create any seven-patch pattern. Two examples are Dove in the Window and Through the Looking Glass (Figures 1-25 and 1-26). Different patch patterns can be used together easily, even when one uses more grid lines than the other (Figure 1-27). Dove in the Window and Through the Looking Glass, two seven-patch patterns, combine to create an intriguing new design (Figure 1-28).

FIGURE 1-26

Through the Looking Glass (seven-patch pattern: 14 x 14 = 196 square grid) (© Joen Wolfrom 1994)

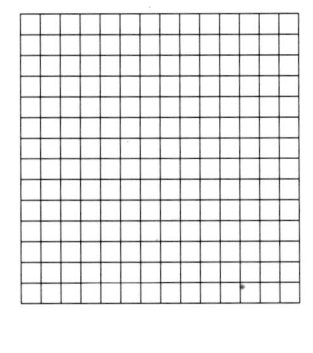

FIGURE 1-23

Some patterns are created by dividing the block into seven equal horizontal and vertical divisions (7 x 7 = 49 square grid).

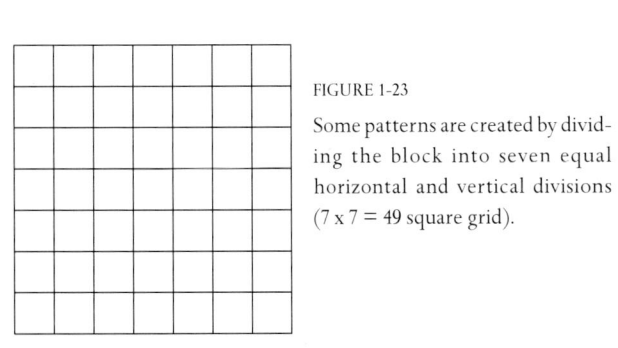

FIGURE 1-27

The two blocks Dove in the Window and Through the Looking Glass fit well together even though the latter pattern has more grid divisions. Because they are both seven-patch patterns, their design lines work together.

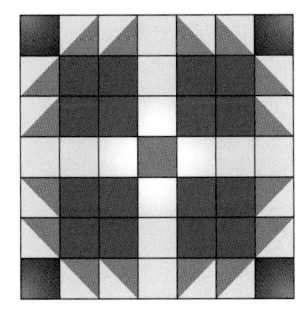

FIGURE 1-24

More complicated seven-patch patterns may need fourteen equal divisions horizontally and vertically (14 x 14 = 196 square grid).

FIGURE 1-25

Dove in the Window (seven-patch pattern: 7 x 7 = 49 square grid)

FIGURE 1-28

Through the Looking Glass and Dove in the Window create an exciting overall design when put together in a nine-block setting.

With few exceptions, combining blocks from unrelated families results in a distracting mixture of mismatched patterns. This happens because the grid lines in each family do not work together. If you are not aware of the unique grid lines of each patch family, you may accidentally mix two patterns from different families. Most likely combining these two designs will be less successful than pairing those that work within their own family. Illusionary Star, a four-patch pattern, and Shoofly, a nine-patch pattern, are unlikely companions because they do not use a similar grid structure (Figure 1-29). Not only can the pattern with the larger divisions overwhelm or outweigh the other block's pattern, but pattern lines and shapes with dissimilar gridding structures do not meet. This causes visual discomfort or gives a busy, confused appearance. An example of this overall design problem is shown in Figure 1-30. For best results when combining two blocks, make certain they are from the same family group, with similarly-placed grid lines and intersecting points. Therefore, nine-patch blocks should be paired with other nine-patch designs; four-patch patterns should be partnered together. If you follow this guideline, you should be successful.

FIGURE 1-29

Illusionary Star, a four-patch pattern, and Shoofly, a nine-patch pattern, are unlikely companions in a quilt setting, because they do not use similar grid lines.

FIGURE 1-30

When patterns from unrelated grid families are combined, the pattern pieces do not meet. Patterns with dissimilar gridding systems, such as these, should not be used. Their combination results in visual confusion and disunity.

Fabric Hints

Choosing fabrics for a quilt is a personal affair. What works for one person may not work for another. Our fabric choices allow for all types of moods, imageries, and suggestive ideas. Drama and subtlety, winter and summer, spring and fall, night and day—all are attainable through our fabric choices. Having a basis for choosing fabrics enables you to rely more easily on your intuition. When the fabrics you choose for a particular quilt meet certain design criteria, you free yourself to follow your instincts in constructing and placing individual blocks.

Generally, fabrics should come together in unity to create the visual statement you wish to make. If one fabric pulls out visually so your eyes are drawn to it without artistic intent, the fabric has either been placed in the design incorrectly or is a poor fabric for the quilt. Either way, it spoils the total effect. If this happens, make a different fabric choice. The most beautiful fabrics use hue, value, intensity, and textural changes to create their designs. Attempt to use fabrics that achieve their major design through these elements.

Use your eyes to choose the best fabrics for your projects. Guide yourself to buy only fabrics that will help you create the imagery you want. If you are uncertain about a certain fabric's visual success, give yourself time to think about it. You may find it is not worth purchasing. Conversely, if you love a fabric that breaks all the guidelines, but you know it will work for you, buy it. The way you incorporate that fabric helps you formulate your own sense of style.

Borders

The purpose of a border is to support, enhance, complete an effect, or give visual closure. A border is not the place to introduce a new idea to a quilt. It is a time for reflection, repetition, and support. This closing quilt feature simply reiterates elements and mirrors parts of the overall design. This reflection may be done through color, fabric, shapes, direction, or patterning. Junko Sawada's *Sunlight and Winds* beautifully illustrates the purpose of a border: reiteration, support, and closure (photo 9A).

If we have to force our eyes to move from the border into the body of the quilt, or if our eyes bounce back and forth from the design to the border, the border treatment is too powerful. If the border is out of proportion to the rest of the design, it seriously competes with the design, often overwhelming it. When this happens, the border becomes dominant, prompting the main attraction to play an insignificant role.

Although not all traditionally pieced quilts need borders, they generally enhance and frame a quilt design so that it looks like a completed work of art. Some quilts, however, are quite fine with just a simple binding. Log Cabin quilts, abstract designs, and landscape quilts are examples of those that may feel encumbered by a border.

BORDER PRINTS AND FABRICS

As a rule of thumb, your border should include prints and hues that have already been introduced in the main body of the quilt. However, sometimes you can successfully use a solid fabric that reiterates the same coloration as an already-included print fabric. Except under careful planning, prints added to the border, which have not been included in the central part of the quilt, can be disastrous, with their incongruity causing distraction. That being said, some quiltmakers have quite successfully broken all rules to create dynamic quilts with wild, wonderful borders. When they do so, they are generally working intuitively and have had experience putting fabrics together in a successful manner.

BORDER SIZE

If you are going to add borders to your quilt, the ratio of block to border is paramount. As a general rule, it is unwise to make each side's border more than one-half the size of your block; less than one-half the block size is often visually preferable. Therefore, if you are working with twelve-inch blocks, it is best to make each side border less than six inches wide. As an option, you may place a small strip of a second border fabric between the pieced border and the main design as an introduction to the border (Figure 1-31A–C). If you do this, the additional strip should be included in the side's border measurement.

A six-inch–wide border is the maximum width for visual balance in a twelve-inch block quilt setting, such as in Hope of Hartford (Figure 1-31A). Here the pieced border's design is equivalent to two grid divisions (slightly less than five inches of a twelve-inch block). The fabric strip separating the body and border is about one inch. In Figure 1-31B the pieced border's width is equal to one and one-half grid divisions (approximately three and one-half inches of a twelve-inch block). The fabric strip adds another inch to its width. A border much narrower than this one, may be out of proportion to the overall design.

In Figure 1-31C the border is larger than half the block's size. This border's oversized width competes visually with the quilt's design. Its shapes are out of proportion to the main design. Thus our eyes jump back and forth from the border to the quilt's design. No shape in the border should be larger than the shapes within the body of the quilt. For instance, if the largest shape in your quilt's design is a four-inch half-square triangle, do not put a six-inch half-square triangle in the border. The border's larger triangle will be out of proportion and will detract from your overall design. You can see this effect in the Figure 1-31C border.

A quilt's beauty can be diminished easily by a poor border. However, if your quilt plan incorporates a well-designed border that reiterates shapes, colors, and fabrics, you should be pleased with your results.

FIGURE 1-31A–C

A quilt's border size plays an important role in the visual success of a quilt. A border's major role is to support, reiterate, enhance, and create closure. The quilt's body and border should have a good visual relationship with each other. The border size plays an important role in design success. It should never be so wide that it competes with the main design visually. Choose a border size that neither looks diminished nor overly strong to work in partnership with your quilt's design.

FIGURE 1-31A

Generally, a border's maximum width should be no more than half the block's size. Additionally, no shape should be larger than any in the quilt's block pattern. This border is the maximum width for this quilt's visual success.

FIGURE 1-31B

In this example, the border is less than half the width of a block. Its width is appropriate for this block setting, because it does not compete visually with the quilt's design. Conversely, the border should not be so narrow that it is out of proportion to the overall design.

FIGURE 1-31C

It is visually unwise to make a border larger than half the width of the block. Likewise, shapes should not be larger than those in the block pattern. When borders are too wide, or shapes are too big, the border is in competition with the design. This is distracting and causes visual disharmony.

1-31A Maximum border size

1-31C Oversized
border and shapes

1-31B Optional border size

FIGURE 1-31A–C

Block to border ratio

CHAPTER TWO ───────────────────────────

Enhancing One-Block Designs

Although we are quite fond of our traditional block patterns, a subtle facelift can be a welcome change for many. This chapter presents the simplest methods to increase your quilt's interest and beauty. All suggestions are easy and small, yet they are effective.

The first step in creating a beautiful quilt is to begin with a well-designed pattern—or at the very least, one you can redesign successfully. It's so much easier to create a beautiful quilt when a pattern has good design qualities than when its visual quality is poor. It behooves us to use patterns that offer the best chance for visual success. Take the time to analyze and play with any pattern you are considering seriously for your quilt. Select one that is worthy of your interest and time.

Knowing Your Pattern— Up Close and Personal

Through past experience I have learned it takes the same amount of time to create an uninteresting quilt as it does a beautiful one. Not knowing how a block reacted to repetition was my biggest error in my early quiltmaking years. I never considered experimenting with the block design on paper before starting a quilt; no one ever suggested I should do so. I assumed each block would automatically result in a beautiful quilt. This naive assumption led to many surprises—several with disappointing results. Since I don't have the time or money to create visually disappointing quilts, it is important for me to be aware of a block's overall de-

sign potential before cutting any fabric. Now I wouldn't dream of beginning a quilt without personal knowledge of how my selected blocks will interact visually.

BLOCK PLAY

Don't let your block selection cause disappointment or unplanned design problems. First, be certain to select a block that will promote a design style that appeals to you. Some blocks look wonderful in isolation, but are rather static in a group setting. Other blocks do not have great appeal alone, but the results are fantastic when several are placed together. Since it is almost impossible to know how a block will interact with other identical blocks by seeing a one-block sample, don't presume to know how quilt blocks go together unless you have actually seen a quilt using the identical blocks. It is essential, then, to begin each quilt project with paper-block play.

Making twenty to thirty small paper blocks (e.g., two-inch blocks) of your selected pattern is one of the wisest planning steps you can make. Then, if the block design doesn't work to your satisfaction, you can choose another block and experiment again. It is far easier to spend a few hours or days playing with paper blocks than to work diligently for a year in fabric and be vastly disappointed with the quilt's end result. Also, you may find your block's design can give great unexpected results if you modify it slightly. This advantageous knowledge is best at the onset of construction rather than in hindsight.

Realizing a Block's Personality Traits

When choosing a block, you can look for several characteristics that may hint at the type of pattern it is, as well as its visual success or disadvantages. Basically, block patterns are either isolated and well defined, or they interact with neighboring blocks to create an overall design. If you know your design style preference, you can choose accordingly.

BLOCK PATTERNS IN ISOLATION

Many people prefer a quilt with a well-defined, isolated block pattern (e.g., *North Carolina Lily,* photo 40A). If you want a design that stands out clearly from the background, look for a block that has its design set away from the block's outside boundary, or choose one where the design has only incidental contact with the outer block edges. With the first, the design is usually centered, as in Dresden Plate (Figure 2-1). The design appears to float above the background. Many star patterns fit into the latter category, with their star points touching the blocks' edges (Figure 2-2A). Although points are touching, the block design does not visually interact with its neighboring blocks very easily (Figure 2-2B).

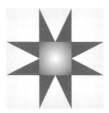

FIGURE 2-2A

Many patterns only have incidental contact with their outer edges. This can cause isolation. Star patterns like Nine-Patch Star fall into this category.

FIGURE 2-2B

A pattern with only incidental contact often creates a static effect in a multiple-block setting. An example can be seen in the Nine-Patch Star quilt.

When a block's design is completely understood or self-contained, as most isolated, well-defined designs are, the quilt's overall design tends to appear rigid or static (Figures 2-3A and B). For some quiltmakers this is a positive feature. For others this rigidity can be a detriment. If you are in the latter group, either choose not to use these patterns or find ways to camouflage these features. A quilt with a camouflaged isolated design is Joy Baaklini's *Milky Way Brocade (*photo 42B). Joy has minimized this static effect by painting diagonal lines on the corner fabrics. This promotes a vibrating movement from each star.

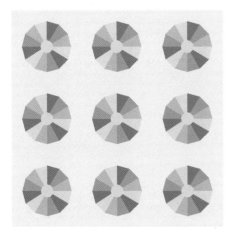

FIGURE 2-1

Generally a block pattern, which has its design set away from its edges, will appear isolated when many blocks are combined. Also, it has the tendency to be static. The Dresden Plate illustrates this isolation and rigidity.

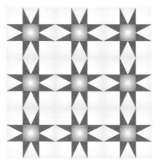

FIGURE 2-3A

Most star patterns are self-contained; therefore they need no neighboring blocks to promote their designs. Illusionary Star is such a pattern (four-patch pattern: 4 x 4 = 16 or 8 x 8 = 64 square grid). (© Joen Wolfrom 1996)

FIGURE 2-3B

In a traditional quilt setting, Illusionary Star gives a static appearance. This is quite prevalent with star patterns, because they do not blend easily with neighboring blocks.

Some blocks have design lines that move beautifully into neighboring blocks, creating interesting designs that blossom in unexpected ways (photo 39B). Many of these patterns automatically create color movement, transparency, and depth. Three block patterns that successfully evolve into overall designs are North Dakota, 1904 Star, and St. Louis Star (Figures 2-4A and B, 2-5A and B, and 2-6A and B). Although these patterns can be quite lovely with traditional color and fabric placement, they have the potential to be stunning when innovatively colored (photo 39A).

FIGURE 2-5B

The 1904 Star pattern can create fleeting circular designs throughout the quilt's surface.

FIGURE 2-4A

North Dakota (four-patch pattern: 8 x 8 = 64 square grid)

FIGURE 2-6A

The St. Louis Star block's design potential is unclear until neighboring blocks are added (nine-patch pattern: 12 x 12 = 144 square grid).

FIGURE 2-4B

FIGURE 2-6B

FIGURE 2-5A

1904 Star (four-patch pattern; 8 x 8 = 64 square grid)

One block characteristic that indicates integration with neighboring blocks is diagonal movement running from corner to corner. Two examples of patterns using diagonal direction to reach beyond the block are Barbara Bannister's Transparent Star and Glowing Stars and Gems (Figures 2-7A and B and 2-8A and B). A beautiful example of block integration with diagonal connections is Katherine Picot's *Free Trade Variation.* Here color and fabric selection has enhanced this integration (photo 39B). Besides diagonal connections, design elements running vertically and horizontally promote movement into neighboring blocks. In Floating Jacks diagonal, vertical, and horizontal design elements flow from one block to another (Figures 2-9A and B). It is possible to create four design layers in this pattern: the foreground jacks, the horizontal and vertical crossbars,

the diagonal stepping stones, and the background. The traditional pattern Vermont has vertical and horizontal movement from one block to the other (Figures 2-10A and B). Transparency and depth can be achieved easily in this pattern.

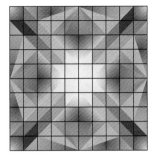

FIGURE 2-8A

Glowing Stars and Gems (five-patch pattern: 10 x 10 = 100 square grid) (© Joen Wolfrom 1991)

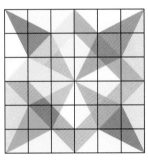

FIGURE 2-7A

Barbara Bannister's Transparent Star (nine-patch pattern: 6 x 6 = 36 square grid) (Variation by Joen Wolfrom 1991)

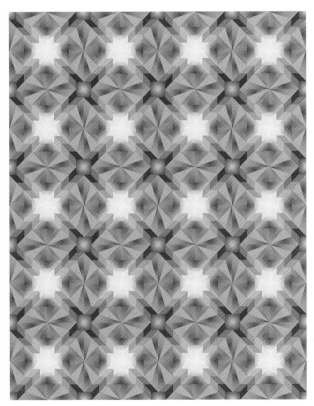

FIGURE 2-8B

Glowing Stars and Gems allows for several design options. Luster, luminosity, transparency, and depth can be achieved with this design.

FIGURE 2-7B

Barbara Bannister's Transparent Star pattern is great for playing with transparency and depth.

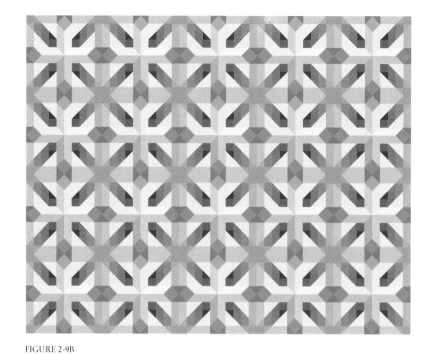

FIGURE 2-9A

Floating Jacks (five-patch pattern: 10 x 10 = 100 square grid)
(© Joen Wolfrom 1991)

FIGURE 2-9B

Floating Jacks can be used to experiment with three-dimensionality, luster, transparency, and even luminosity.

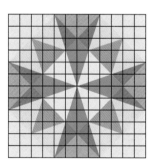

FIGURE 2-10A

Vermont (nine-patch pattern: 12 x 12 = 144 square grid)

FIGURE 2-10B

Vermont can be used to create the illusions of depth, transparency, luminosity, and luster.

PATTERNS WITH ACTIVE PERSONALITIES

Many patterns can change their personality and design focus simply from the way you choose to work with fabrics and colors. The options are endless, and the outcome of your design can be a mystery until the last blocks are created and put in place (photos 40B, 42A and C). One such block is Curved Pathways (Figure 2-11A). Two views have been created to show how readily the design can change with the color placement. The first design uses identical color placement throughout the design. Its design appears more pronounced and somewhat rigid (Figure 2-11B). In Figure 2-11C the colors and values are closely related, but because there are subtle changes in the block, the star tends to disappear with the curving movement in this Curved Pathways design (Figure 2-11D). Gem Stone is a similar pattern. I designed it so that movement, transparency, shadows, and highlights would be possible to achieve (Figure 2-12A). With identical blocks (Figure 2-12B) the movement is less effective than if each block had its own unique coloring.

 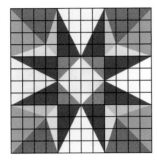

FIGURE 2-11A

Curved Pathways (four-patch pattern: 8 x 8 = 64 or 12 x 12 = 144 square grid) (© Joen Wolfrom 1981)

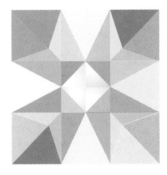

FIGURE 2-11C

By muting the colors and keeping the values closely related, Curved Pathways changes subtly.

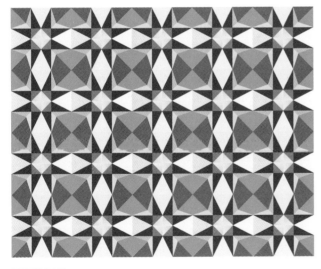

FIGURE 2-11B

There are many illusionary possibilities with the pattern Curved Pathways. In this traditional setting, the repetitive color plan creates a design with the stars prominently displayed.

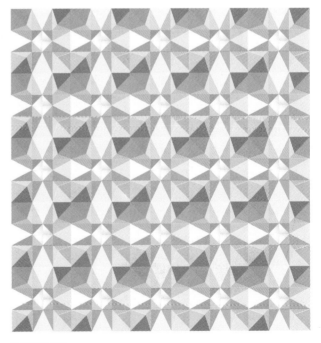

FIGURE 2-11D

With muted colors and subtle value changes, a curved movement becomes apparent. Numerous curved pathways are created; the star is less pronounced.

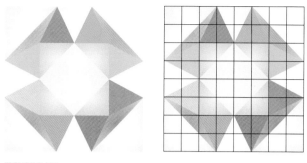

FIGURE 2-12A

Gem Stone (four-patch pattern: 8 x 8 = 64 square grid) (© Joen Wolfrom 1981)

Storm at Sea, a very popular pattern, continues to pique our interest because of its diverse design possibilities (Figures 2-13A and B). The design effects can be changed dramatically by color and fabric use. The key to making these successful quilts is to use a large variety of fabrics. This results in a scrap-quilt look. Maureen McGee and Sara Dickson joined together to make their own intriguing Storm at Sea quilt (photo 69A). Mary Gillis, fascinated by the illusion of curves in designs like Storm at Sea, has created *Call Me, Moby* (photo 69B).

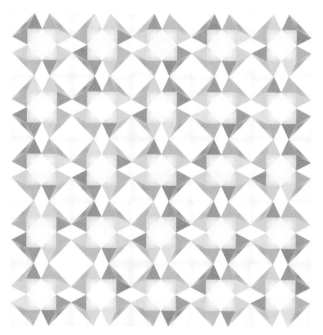

FIGURE 2-12B

In this color plan, the gem stones are fairly static. However, if colors and values are closely related, as in Figure 2-11D, meandering circular pathways appear, and the design changes considerably.

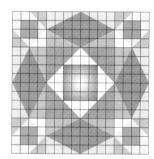

FIGURE 2-13A

Storm at Sea (four-patch pattern: 8 x 8 = 64 or 16 x 16 = 256 square grid)

FIGURE 2-13B

Storm at Sea is one of the most popular traditional patterns because there are so many design possibilities that can be created. Here the sea wave movement is very apparent in the overall design.

The Kaleidoscope block has great design potential (Figure 2-14). Sharla Hicks' two Kaleidoscope quilts vary greatly in *Adam's Outer Realm* and *Ruel's Kaleidoscope* (photos 41C and 7B). Sharla did not work with individual blocks. Instead, she used the blocks' pattern pieces to create color movement, shifting the colors across the design surface. She worked from a design wall, placing fabrics on its surface piece by piece. Marion Marias worked in similar fashion with her *Contemporary Kaleidoscope* (photo 42C). Her color and value play ended with quite different results. With the Kaleidoscope pattern, quilters can create amazingly different designs as Donna Schneider did in *Plaid, Sweat, and Tears* (photo 41D).

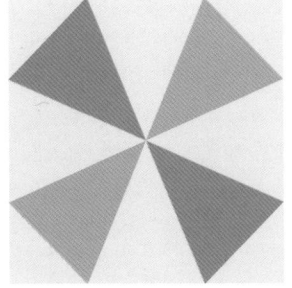

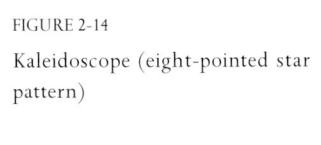

FIGURE 2-14

Kaleidoscope (eight-pointed star pattern)

Using Fabrics and Colors to Increase a Pattern's Interest

Historically, we have been taught to make quilts with identical fabric use in each block. This practice made sense when fabrics were difficult to purchase and when there were few fabric choices. However, with our bountiful fabric selection today, simple quilt designs can zing and stimulate our senses when we use a multitude of fabrics. If you incorporate fabrics with a wide variety of prints, textures, patterns, values, intensities, and subtle color changes, each block will be unique and intriguing. When the quilt is complete, it will sparkle with interesting pattern, texture, and color play.

An easy way to add dramatic interest to your quilt is to change the background fabrics subtly (Figures 2-4B, 2-7B, 2-11D, and 2-12B and photos 8A, B, and C). If you decide to use blue for your quilt's background, don't use just one fabric; instead, use many blue fabrics. These fabrics do not need to match. Color, value, and intensity differences add to a design's beauty. Subtle clashing intensifies our interest. Ten, fifteen, or perhaps thirty different fabrics could be incorporated in your quilt's background.

Your fabrics can be placed in a serendipitous fashion or in a very prescribed manner, depending on the effect you wish to create. The diagonal setting of Nine-Patch Star illustrates a subtle value change in background fabrics (Figure 2-15D). Subtle changes in value, intensity, pattern, and hue can give your background an incredible effect. It can evoke the illusions of highlights, shadows, transparency, and depth (Figures 3-14, 4-11, 5-11, 5-12, 5-13, 6-9, 6-14, 6-15, 6-16, 6-21B, and 7-1A and B; photos 7A, 8A, 9A, 12B, 14A, 70A, 73A, 77B, 81A, 83A, 84A, 101C, and 121A and C).

The same color, value, and fabric changes may be made for the foreground design elements in your blocks. Again, use a wide variety of fabrics in your chosen color scheme. This will increase interest and cause the eye to see new areas of intrigue each time the quilt is viewed (photos 100A, and 40B). Arlene Stamper's *Koinonia Garden* is a lovely example of changing foreground fabrics. Her lilies are beautifully colored in a multitude of hues (photo 11A). Rosey Hunt has used dozens of fabrics to create the interlocking wave effect in her *She's All at Sea* quilt (photo 13C). Transparency has been achieved through subtle fabric changes. Illustrations showing other subtle color changes in foreground patterns include Figures 2-4B, 2-7B, and 2-11D. Quilts with subtle foreground fabric and color changes include 10A, 11A, 12A, 16B, 16C, 40B, 41D, 73B, 74A and B, 76B, 77B, 80C, 83A, and 125B.

Using a Block's Pattern to Create an Unrelated Design

There may be times when you use the block design to create something extraordinarily different from the actual block pattern (photos 7B, 14B, 15B, and 41A, B, and C). In this case, the pattern pieces are simply tools to work with. A quilt based on this concept is quite imaginative. You may want to play with a color illusion. Using pattern pieces as a vehicle allows you freedom to do so. Or you may wish to create a representative picture, ignoring the block completely. Creating a completely different design from the traditional block expectation can be fun, and it will stretch your imagination. Do not be afraid to be adventurous with your block play. When constructing the design, either sew the blocks together in the traditional method, or construct the design in rows, eliminating the block altogether.

The Storm at Sea pattern lends itself to innovative design play. One example is Sue Atlas's imaginative quilt *Beauty and the Beast* (photo 42A). The traditional design is no longer recognizable. Through color and fabric manipulation, the pattern pieces have created a scene. The sun, water, hills, mountains, and sky were created by using the block's pattern pieces as design tools to create a fantasy landscape.

WORKING ON YOUR INNOVATIVE DESIGN

You can plan your own innovative quilt by drawing your quilt's outline to scale on paper. Draw and color your desired picture within the quilt's boundary. Then divide the picture into squares. These squares represent individual blocks. Select a block pattern that will allow you to manipulate colors easily. It should not be too difficult to construct. Generally, it is best to stay away from blocks with intricate, small pieces.

When you make an unrelated design with a traditional block pattern, your pattern evolves step by step. It can be very intuitive. If possible, work from a design wall or board. Stand back to observe your progress often. It is difficult to assess your design accurately when you are working only a few inches away from it.

Enhancing the Design—Using a Diagonal Setting

Placing traditional blocks in a diagonal setting often enhances the design or adds pizzazz to your quilt's overall design. Floral appliquéd and pieced patterns are particularly beautiful in diagonal settings. A lovely example is Cynthia England's *North Carolina Lily* (photo 40A). If a diagonal setting enhances your block design's visual appeal, think about incorporating this simple pattern change. The static Nine-Patch Star (Figure 2-15A) is given a face-lift when put in a diagonal setting (Figure 2-15D).

During your quilt's planning stage, take your paper blocks and arrange them diagonally. See if you prefer this setting. If you work with a diagonal setting, determine how you will plan for the corners and side spaces. Will you include partial blocks? Will you add another dimension to your design? Or will you let the design float above the background, as is done in Figure 2-15D? If the diagonal setting appeals to you, make certain you tailor your blocks' size to your desired overall dimensions.

DIAGONAL BLOCKS GAIN GIRTH

If you use a diagonal setting and do not adjust the block's size, your quilt will grow appreciably. If you planned a traditional setting in a specific size, and then decide to use a diagonal setting, you must change your block's dimensions to keep the quilt at its originally-planned size. This sizing becomes important because a square's dimension changes when measured from one side to another side compared to when measured from one corner to another (Figures 2-15A, B, and C). The diagonal measurement decidedly increases the block's size (Figure 2-15C). If you rotate the block to a diagonal setting, and you want to maintain the same horizontal and vertical block measurement, you must diminish the actual block size (Figure 2-15B).

If you keep the same block size, and you want to know how much this rotated setting will increase your quilt's dimensions, you can either measure your block corner to corner or figure the measurement mathematically by using the Pythagorean theorem (an easy formula we used in high school geometry class). To figure your needed dimensions, multiply your block size by the square root of two (1.414).

If you have a ten-inch block, simply multiply its size by 1.414. Thus, 10 inches x 1.414 = 14.14 inches. Your ten-inch block will be approximately fourteen inches wide in a diagonal setting. This is a considerable increase—a little over four inches! With this in mind, be certain to take this increase into consideration during your planning stage. If you do not want this increase, decrease the block size to coincide with your desired quilt dimensions. Although it is quite easy to do this arithmetic, the following chart gives you the conversion block-size when you change to a diagonal setting.

Block Size	*Diagonal Measurement*	
2" block	2.82"	(approx. 2⅞")
3" block	4.24"	(approx. 4¼")
4" block	5.65"	(approx. 5⅝")
5" block	7.07"	(approx. 7 1/16")
6" block	8.48"	(approx. 8½")
7" block	9.89"	(approx. 9 15/16")
8" block	11.31"	(approx. 11 5/16")
9" block	12.72"	(approx. 12¾")
10" block	14.14"	(approx. 14⅛")
11" block	15.55"	(approx. 15 9/16")
12" block	16.97"	(approx. 17")
13" block	18.38"	(approx. 18⅜")
14" block	19.79"	(approx. 19¾")
15" block	21.21"	(approx. 21 7/32")
16" block	22.62"	(approx. 22⅝")
17" block	24.04"	(approx. 24")
18" block	25.45"	(approx. 25½")
19" block	26.87"	(approx. 26⅞")
20" block	28.28"	(approx. 28¼")
22" block	31.11"	(approx. 31⅛")
24" block	33.94"	(approx. 33 15/16")
25" block	35.35"	(approx. 35⅜")

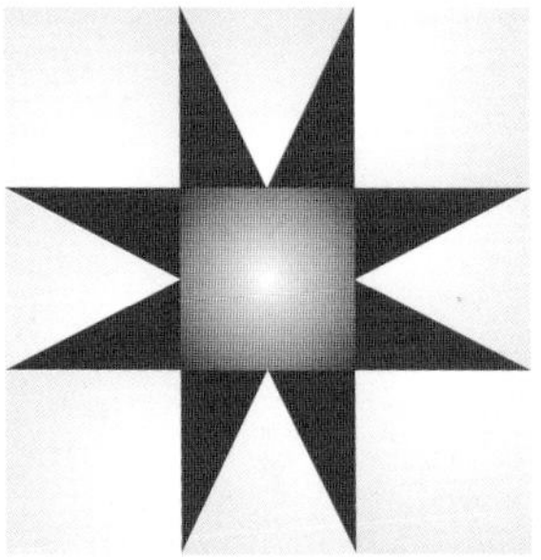

FIGURE 2-15A

Nine-Patch Star (nine-patch pattern: 6 x 6 = 36 square grid)

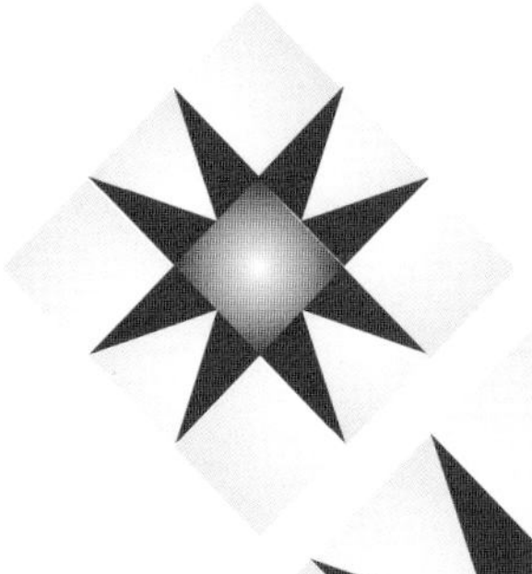

FIGURE 2-15B

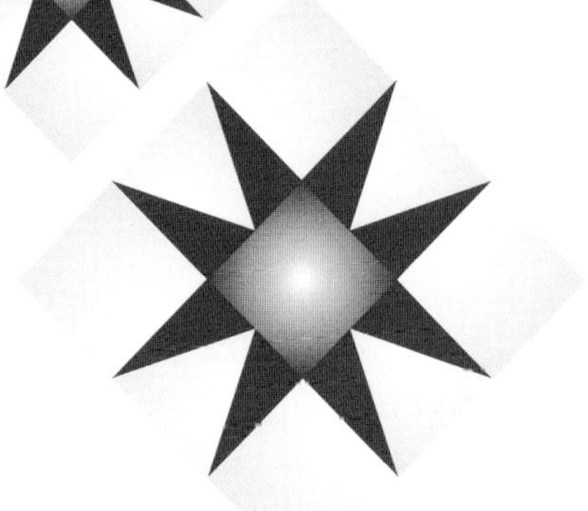

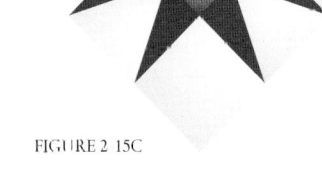

FIGURE 2-15C

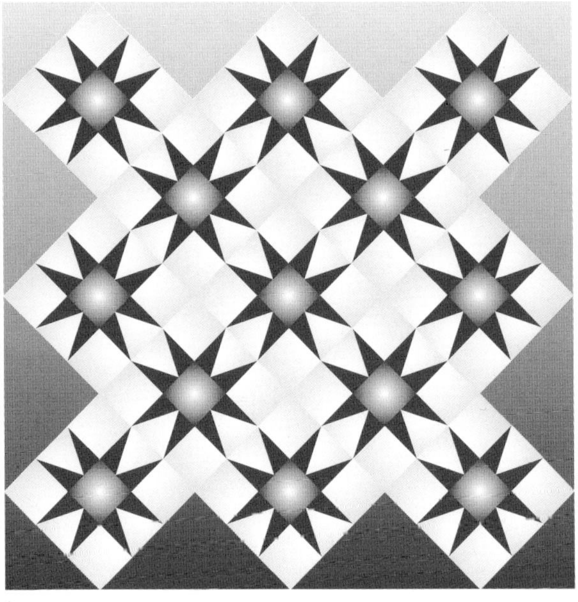

FIGURE 2-15D

When the Nine-Patch Star is placed in a diagonal setting, the design takes on a different appearance from its usual setting (Figure 2-2B). Here it is more interesting.

Activities and Extended Learning

1. Choose a pattern. Make thirty to forty paper copies of the block with a copy machine or computer (2" to 3" blocks). Then make a paper quilt using the traditional block setting. Glue the blocks to a paper background. Then make a second paper quilt setting the blocks diagonally. Be innovative with your setting; don't assume it must be in the traditional diagonal format. You will have to cut apart a few blocks to finish edges and corners. Glue in place.

Notice the diagonally-set paper quilt is larger than the traditional setting. Figure what size block you should begin with in order to have it come out the same size as the first quilt. Which setting pleases you more?

39A. *Canyon Echoes,* 1995, 72" x 72"
Beth Gilbert, Buffalo Grove, Illinois

This wonderful quilt was created
because of the enchantment Beth felt
after a trip to the southwest. The cliff
dwellings in Mesa Verde, Colorado,
inspired the beautifully muted
coloration of *Canyon Echoes.* Photo:
Courtesy of the artist

39B. *Free Trade Variation,* 1987, 48½" x 48½"
Katherine Picot, Bühl, Germany

Because of the way Katherine used colors and fabrics in this
variation of Free Trade, this quilt appears to be made from
two different block patterns. Surprisingly, however, it is
not. One must observe the quilt carefully to see the block
definition. The result of Katherine's efforts is a lovely quilt
of subtle beauty. Photo: Franz Silzner

40A. *North Carolina Lily*, 1986, 56" x 72"
Cynthia England, Houston, Texas

Cynthia was inspired to make this quilt after seeing the North Carolina Lily tapestry on her sofa fabric. She pulled the colors from that fabric. It is pieced and appliquéd. This pattern is lovely in an on-point (diagonal) setting. Photo: Ken Wagner

40B. *Sazanami (Water Rings)*, 1991, 86½" x 86½"
Junko Sawada, Yokohama-shi, Japan

Junko often uses traditional patterns as her initial inspiration. This quilt, based on the Double Wedding Ring pattern, brings to Junko's mind the illusion of the azure and purple hydrangeas reflected in a pool of water under a rainy gray sky in June. The subtle fabric and color changes are unbelievable close up. Junko has exquisitely hand pieced and hand quilted *Sazanami*. Photo: Carina Woolrich

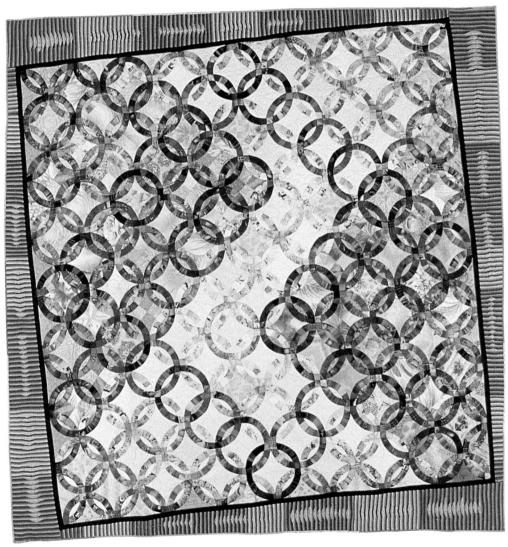

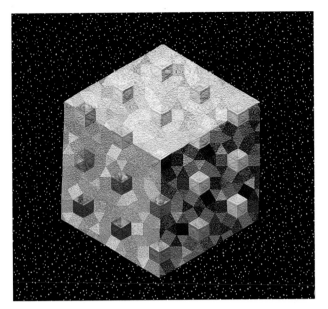

41A. *Oblique Illusion,* 1992, 50" x 50"
Martie Huston, Santee, California

Martie has taken the traditional block pattern Jack's Chain and created an unbelievably innovative rendition. In fact, one has to study this quilt closely to see the Jack's Chain block. It is a superb example of using a block's shapes to create an entirely different vision. Photo: Ken Wagner

41B. *Persian Plenty,* 1995, 103" x 118"
Joan Dyer, Redondo Beach, California

A wedding quilt made for her daughter; Joan uses the traditional Nine-Patch Basket block to create this dynamic design. Photo: Jack Mathieson

41C. *Adam's Outer Realm,* 1994, 70" x 80"
Sharla Hicks, Anaheim, California

Using the Kaleidoscope block, Sharla created her quilt with an innovative interpretation. She designed her quilt with the single shapes within the block. She continued to play with the placement of shapes until she felt the design was balanced. Photo: Courtesy of the artist

41D. *Plaid, Sweat, and Tears,* 1994, 49" x 60"
Donna Schneider, Kelowna, British Columbia, Canada

This quilt is part of a set of plaid quilts called "Plaid-itudes." This Kaleidoscope quilt was inspired by Lois Monieson's quilt shown in the April 1993 issue of *Quilter's Newsletter Magazine.* Although Lois' colors are carefully arranged and balanced, Donna decided to create a scrap quilt with stars and plaids forming circles in no definite color pattern. Photo: Ken Wagner

42A. *Beauty and the Beast*, 1993, 40" x 40"
Susan Atlas, Lakeside, California

The Storm at Sea block was used as the foundation to create this scene. Susan created this design in a Stretching Traditions workshop given by the author. The design proved so intriguing that Susan decided to make a quilt from it. Photo: Ken Wagner

42B. *Milky Way Brocade*, 1987, 52" x 52"
Joy Baaklini, Austin, Texas

This quilt was made from hand-painted two-inch squares, which were pieced into six-inch blocks. The hard-edge painting was achieved using masking tape and opalescent fabric paint. The contrast between the hard edges of the geometric shapes and the fluid waving lines, which overlay the subtle patterns of the printed fabrics, is fascinating. Photo: Ken Wagner

42C. *Contemporary Kaleidoscope*, 1990, 52" x 64"
Marion Marias, Bend, Oregon

Marion made this quilt by first sewing strip panels; then cutting triangles from these panels, using the 45-degree kaleidoscope wedge ruler. These triangles were sewn into octagons. Corner triangles were added to complete the block. Light values were placed in the upper left. The values changed gradually into darker colors as the design moved to the lower areas of the quilt. Owner: Kristen Frey. Photo: Ken Wagner

CHAPTER THREE

Superb Block Marriages—Blends and Merges

Over the years quiltmakers have combined two different blocks to make new, more interesting quilt patterns. The results can be dynamic, if blocks are well paired. One of the most important considerations when combining blocks is to choose patterns which are compatible in their makeup. To be harmonious the blocks must come from the same family roots (page 20). Then the blocks' patterns will have the same grid lines, reference lines, and reference points. Although there are several methods to bring different blocks together, my two favorite ways are *blending* and *merging*. Each has the capability to create wonderful original designs. (Please read Anatomy of a Quilt Block, beginning on page 19, prior to working with the concepts in this chapter.)

Blending Blocks

When we blend two blocks together, our goal is to combine them harmoniously, so the patterns appear to bleed gradually into one another. With successful blending the blocks should not be distinguished from each other easily. In effect, both blocks lose some or all of their individual definition and a new design results. Often the blended design appears more intricate than a one-block design. There is continuity throughout the quilt's surface.

Besides choosing patterns which are related in grid make-up, select blocks you think will create a visually interesting or beautiful quilt. Choosing two blocks can be a risky activity. There are times when it is impossible to predict how two blocks will react to each other. Sometimes you make a lucky choice; at other times, it may take several selections before you have a winning combination.

Attempt to have some of the design lines of one block lead into the adjoining blocks' lines, thereby making a visual connection. Look for patterns that appear to move their designs outward. Possibly use one block that has potential diagonal movement. This can enhance the blocks' unification. This happens with Spinning Stars and Wild Duck (Figures 3-1, 3-2, 3-3A and B). Examples of quilts made from two blocks that blend together are *My Spring Vignettes* by Lynn Underwood and *Tennessee Waltz* by Diane Ebner (photos 57A and 58A).

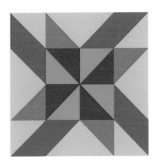 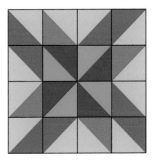

FIGURE 3 1

Spinning Stars (four-patch pattern: 4 x 4 = 16 square grid)

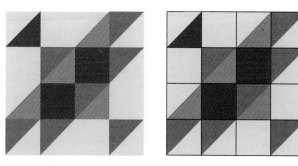

FIGURE 3-2

Wild Duck (four-patch pattern: 4 x 4 = 16 square grid)

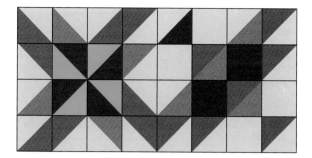

FIGURE 3-3A

When combining two blocks, attempt to have one block's design lines move into another block's design. This will unite the blocks into an interlocking blend.

FIGURE 3-3B

Because Wild Duck's and Spinning Star's design lines fit well together, their union results in an interesting pattern. Many other design possibilities are available by changing the colors used.

UNSUCCESSFUL BLENDS

If the blocks remain individual patterns when placed together in a quilt setting, they have not been blended. Nor does incidental interaction create blending. Blocks with large open spaces in the corners are difficult to blend, as this characteristic readily promotes design isolation (Figures 3-4 and 3-5). Star and Squares and Shooting Star decline to blend when placed together because each has only incidental contact with the other (Figure 3-6).

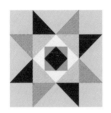 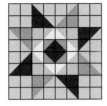

FIGURE 3-4

Star and Squares (four-patch pattern: 8 x 8 = 16 square grid)

 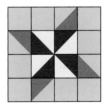

FIGURE 3-5

Shooting Star (four-patch pattern: 4 x 4 = 16 square grid)

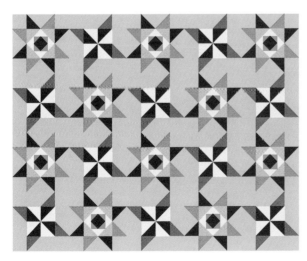

FIGURE 3-6

Two blocks with large open corner areas often create isolated block designs rather than block blends. These can lead to disappointing results, as no real blending has occurred.

If you want to use two isolated patterns to create a blended effect, consider drawing additional design lines to eliminate the isolating characteristics. In Figure 3-7A Shooting Star has had design lines extended into its corners. Altering the block this way creates an interesting lattice around the Star and Square pattern (Figure 3-7B).

 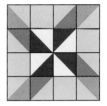

FIGURE 3-7A

Shooting Star Variation. The outer corners of Shooting Star have been changed to eliminate the large corner squares and open areas.

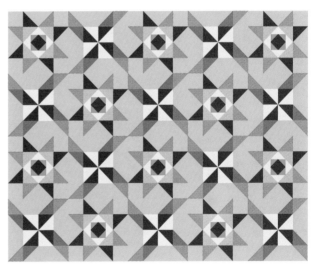

FIGURE 3-7B

By making the small line change in the Shooting Star corner squares (Figure 3-7A), the block is better partnered with the pattern Star and Squares. Other alternatives could have been chosen with equally good results.

Two simple patterns can make great partners, so do not neglect looking at relatively uncomplicated patterns for your design inspiration. For example, Churn Dash and Balkan Puzzle are two simple four-patch patterns (Figure 3-8 and 3-9). When combined, they blend into an interesting geometric design with a multitude of optical illusions possible (Figure 3-10). Color ideas are endless. Diane Ebner's *Tennessee Waltz* is a perfect example of using two relatively simple patterns (photo 58A). She has combined the simple Snowball block with a 54-40 or Fight block. This combination was inspired by a quilt in Judy Martin's *Scrap Quilts* book (see Sources).

Combining a simple pattern with a more complicated one can be a difficult feat, although not an impossible one. Often these joinings do not result in true blends. Instead, the one with the larger pattern pieces is usually emphasized while the other plays a lesser role. However, the two block patterns should enhance each other. If they do not, then find a way to encourage their blending.

Combining two intricate patterns can be stunning, if the patterns mutually enhance each other. *Red Hot Chili Peppers* by Sylvia Kundrats is a great example of blending two blocks (photo 57B). Sylvia's center block is from Doreen Speckmann's *Pattern Play* (see Sources). The second block is a variation Sylvia made from Mrs. Bryant's Choice. Both are nine-patch patterns. Sylvia has extended the quilt by adding a one-third section of the block around the outside perimeter. Her extension of the four large diamonds adds visual interest to the design.

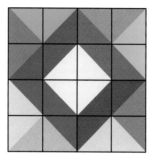

FIGURE 3-8

Churn Dash (four-patch pattern: 4 x 4 = 16 square grid)

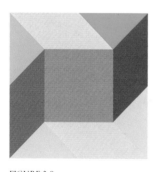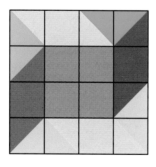

FIGURE 3-9

Balkan Puzzle (four-patch pattern: 4 x 4 = 16 square grid)

FIGURE 3-10

Simple block patterns can be successfully combined. Strong geometric designs can be created by having the blocks' design lines move from one block to another.

CREATING FASCINATING BLENDS

The Nine-Patch Star is a workhorse block because its simple design can be altered easily (Figure 3-11). The nine-patch pattern Storm at Sea is less well known than the four-patch pattern of the same name (Figure 3-12). When the two nine-patch patterns are paired, a joyful design materializes (Figure 3-13). If careful fabric choices are made, a slight circular design will occur with this partnership. The circular motion is more apparent when the pair is put on-point (Figure 3-14).

When this Storm at Sea is combined with St. Louis Star, quite a different design evolves (Figures 3-15A, B, and C). Again, the possibility of a subtle circular design is slightly hinted at with this blend. Transparency may easily be achieved, too.

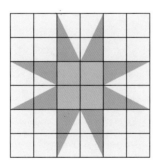

FIGURE 3-11
Nine-Patch Star (nine-patch pattern: 6 x 6 = 36 square grid)

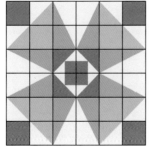

FIGURE 3-12
Storm at Sea (nine-patch pattern: 6 x 6 = 36 square grid)

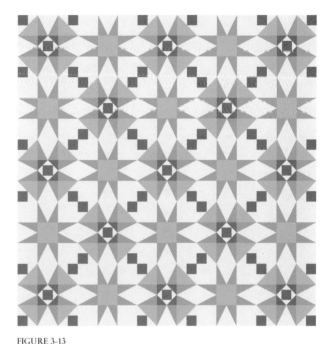

FIGURE 3-13
The Nine-Patch Star and Storm at Sea blocks combine to create a blended design.

FIGURE 3-14
When the Nine-Patch Star and Storm at Sea blocks are set diagonally, the design changes slightly. The subtle circular movement can be enhanced by fabric placement.

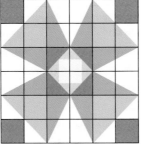

FIGURE 3-15A

Storm at Sea (nine-patch pattern: 6 x 6 = 36 square grid)

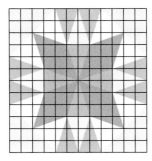

FIGURE 3-15B

St. Louis Star (nine-patch pattern: 6 x 6 = 36 or 12 x 12 = 144 square grid)

FIGURE 3-15C

The blend of Storm at Sea and St. Louis Star creates a wonderful over-all design. Subtle circular and curved designs appear. Even transparency is enhanced.

Do not overlook blending simple patterns. With clever color and fabric presentation, great designs can evolve. Here Nine-Patch Square and Box Quilt create an interesting interplay (Figures 3-16, 17, and 18). Different color plans will give this blended partnership many personality changes.

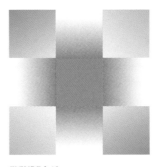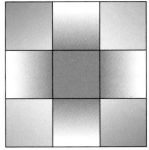

FIGURE 3-16

Nine-Patch Square (nine-patch pattern: 3 x 3 = 9 square grid)

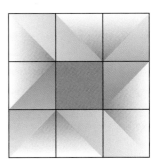

FIGURE 3-17

Box Quilt (nine-patch pattern: 3 x 3 = 9 square grid)

FIGURE 3-18

Uncomplicated patterns can make good partners in block blends. Here the Nine-Patch Square is combined with Box Quilt to create a graphic design with a contemporary flair.

PLAYING WITH MORE BLENDS

The overall effect may not be immediately apparent when joining any two blocks. With a little block play, the design begins to evolve. Surprising results can happen. Figuring out how to place the blocks in the quilt is part of the fun of creating the quilt. Don't assume you must alternate the blocks. Perhaps you will use one block more than another. In Figure 3-19C, the nine-patch Storm at Sea has been combined with Dublin Steps (Figures 3-19A and B). After many alterations the final plan resulted in the Storm at Sea being surrounded by Dublin Steps.

Work innovatively. Give yourself time to play before making a final decision about which blocks to use and how they will be placed in your quilt.

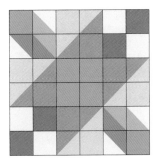

FIGURE 3-19A

Storm at Sea (nine-patch pattern: 6 x 6 = 36 square grid)

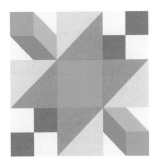

FIGURE 3-19B

Dublin Steps (nine-patch pattern: 6 x 6 = 36 square grid)

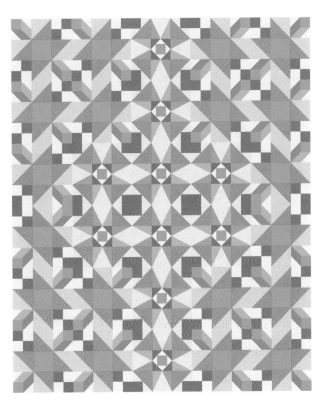

FIGURE 3-19C

A block partnership can include unusual or unexpected block placement. Here the blocks are not alternated; instead one block pattern surrounds the other.

Do not feel compelled to keep your blocks in straight lines, resulting in expected placements. Unexpected results may occur when you set your blended blocks together diagonally. Let you mind discover new placement ideas. Do not discount good ideas simply because you are unsure of how to draft, construct, or quilt them. Each step can be dealt with successfully, one step at a time.

Color can play a very important part in your blended design. To illustrate this, 1904 Star is shown in two different color combinations with the four-patch Storm at Sea pattern. The first shows a simple blending of the two blocks (Figures 3-20A, B, and C). In the second example the 1904 Star has two color variations (Figures 3-21B and C). Randomly placing the differently colored 1904 Star blocks in the design with Storm at Sea (Figure 3-21A), has made a free-spirited design (Figure 3-21D).

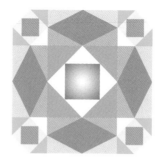 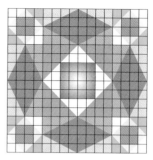

FIGURE 3-20A

Storm at Sea (four-patch pattern: 8 x 8 = 64 or 16 x 16 = 256 square grid)

 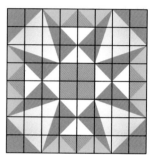

FIGURE 3-20B

1904 Star (four-patch pattern: 8 x 8 = 64 square grid)

FIGURE 3-20C

Using Storm at Sea and 1904 Star, the blocks are blended into an interesting design when similar colors are used. Subtle fabric variations can create added interest.

FIGURE 3-21A

This Storm at Sea block can blend easily to create innovative designs.

FIGURE 3-21B

1904 Star will join Storm at Sea in a more free-flowing design.

FIGURE 3-21C

The 1904 Star looks quite different with another color combination.

FIGURE 3-21D

Blending Storm at Sea with two color variations of 1904 Star, which are randomly placed throughout the surface area, results in a free-flowing, spontaneous design.

Other blended block combinations are shown in the Anatomy of a Quilt Block section beginning on page 19. Shoofly and Card Tricks are two simple blocks that create a very nice blend (Figure 1-11, page 20). Through the Looking Glass and Dove in the Window make a great blend and an exciting design (Figure 1-28, page 23). As you can see, combining two or more patterns can be wonderful fun, as well as a means to create dynamic designs.

Quilts can be blended in many different ways. An exquisite example of blending blocks is shown in *Sunlight and Winds* by Junko Sawada (photo 9A). She has used lily and basket blocks to create her surface design. Additionally, she has appliquéd leaves and stems for her lilies and flowers, and individual petals, to create a feeling of freedom. Junko's border beautifully supports her overall design, reiterating colors and shapes within the quilt while providing closure.

Be willing to experiment, so you can create the best possible setting for your block combination. After you determine your block selection, make several copies of each on a copy machine or your computer. Have at least fifteen to twenty small paper blocks of each pattern, so you do not limit your design options. Play with several options. If your two chosen blocks do not interact well, replace one of the blocks. Then continue your design play until you are satisfied.

Merging Patterns Through Block Explosion

If you enjoy working with two different blocks in a quilt design, you may wish to increase the challenge by creating a design that breaks apart the two blocks and then unites them by using parts of each. The result is unlike the blending of two blocks. Although blending and merging are related, they are quite different in concept. Blending uses each block as a whole entity. Merging requires the blocks be broken apart and then repositioned together in new combinations. The two blocks become united in a new design. It seems as if each block explodes; the pieces come together in a union that previously did not exist.

In many ways the concept of merging is similar to the way a child reflects her parents. The child is not a replica of either parent; instead, she is a unique combination of both. Merging is similar in concept. After selecting the parent blocks, break their shapes into individual pieces and combination units. Then put these together uniquely. Merging is a tool for bringing us greater freedom to explore design possibilities while keeping within certain traditional parameters.

To illustrate this concept, the two blocks Nine-Patch Star and Crossing Triangles were chosen as merging partners (Figures 3-22A and B). Parts of each block were separated into pattern units or individual pieces (Figure 3-22C). Then these were used in various combinations to create a new design. Figure 3-22D shows the beginning stage of a merged design using whole blocks along with pattern pieces and units of Nine-Patch Star and Crossing Triangles. As you can imagine, the possible design combinations are almost endless. *Blue Ice Dance* (page 54) is one design that was created through the merging of these two blocks (Figure 3-22E). The beginning of another merged design using the same two blocks (Figure 3-23A) and their pattern units can be seen in Figure 3-23B, *Star Light, Star Bright*.

Merging is an exciting new way to work with traditional blocks. I encourage you to create your own original designs using the concept of merged-block designs. Endless patterns are available to use as your starting point in designing a merged-block quilt.

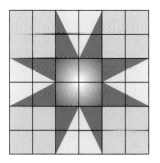

FIGURE 3-22A

Nine-Patch Star (nine-patch pattern: 6 x 6 = 36 square grid)

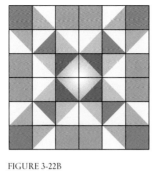

FIGURE 3-22B

Crossing Triangles (nine-patch pattern: 6 x 6 = 36 square grid) (© Joen Wolfrom 1992)

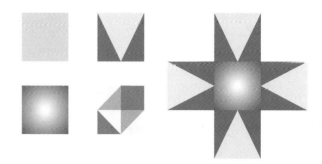

FIGURE 3-22C

To merge, the blocks are broken into small units or solitary pieces. These are grouped together in a different manner to establish a new design. Some block parts used to create *Blue Ice Dance* are shown in Figures 3-22D and E.

FIGURE 3-22D

The beginning stage of a merged design using Nine-Patch Star and Crossing Triangles is shown here.

FIGURE 3-22E

The process of taking two block patterns apart internally and rear-ranging their parts into a new design results in merging. By using the two blocks Nine-Patch Star and Crossing Triangles in whole block, unit, and individual shape combinations, the new design *Blue Ice Dance* was created.

FIGURE 3-23A

Nine-Patch Star and Crossing Triangles have been taken apart in order to create a merged design.

FIGURE 3-23B

By playing with the various parts of Nine-Patch Star and Crossing Triangles, *Star Light, Star Bright* has been created.

If you want to create a merged design, the first step will be to select your blocks. Although you should use only two blocks for your first merged quilt, later you may challenge yourself by using three or more block patterns. These selected blocks should have a common relationship in their gridding. Therefore, make certain they are from the same pattern family (page 19). If you do not follow this guideline, you will struggle with getting the various pattern pieces to fit together. In fact, it may be impossible.

Make several paper copies of each selected block pattern. Next, cut the pattern pieces apart. Using the block copies, cut various pattern combinations from both block patterns. These will be your pattern units, or pattern modules. Each unit has its own personality. They work together like pieces of a puzzle.

Begin your design wherever you feel most comfortable—or wherever your design dictates you begin. Remember, there is no *right way*. As you work, place your first selection on white paper. Then begin building a design by positioning the various design parts onto the paper. Continue to add whole and partial blocks or pattern units to already-positioned pieces. When creating the design, attempt to let the design evolve without too much analyzing. Give room to the background, so it can support the design adequately. Part of the white paper below the design can be designated as background space if you want to create additional background space in your design. This background will be constructed with fillers, which can be made from pattern units or geometric shapes.

Make enough pattern copies to have several overall design options from which to choose. While playing, change your ideas and experiment as much as you like. If you have an illustration program on your computer, you will be able to make many design variations with considerable ease. Eventually you will gravitate to one or two ideas that really excite you. After choosing your favorite, glue the pattern to paper. This will be your *construction map*.

Determine the size you wish your quilt to be. From this measurement, and the number of blocks that fit across your design, determine the block size. For example, if you want a sixty-inch–wide quilt, and you have created a design that incorporates five horizontal blocks, you will need to draft twelve-inch blocks (60 divided by 5 = 12). After you have drafted your blocks, make the templates using your favorite template material. Label the templates with the block's name, size, and other pertinent information. You can construct your quilt in a block format, or you can sew the pieces together in rows. For merging blocks, I prefer constructing the quilt in rows. Use your construction map to follow your design plan.

Activities and Extended Learning

1. Choose two blocks to blend together. Make certain they have a structural relationship. Make fifteen to twenty copies of each block. Blend the two blocks into a quilt design. When you have created a design that excites you, glue it on paper. Begin planning this future quilt.

2. Choose two blocks to merge. Make certain they have a structural relationship. Make fifteen to twenty copies of each block. Begin cutting the block pieces apart. Start arranging their parts into a design. When you are happy with an arrangement, glue the pieces in place. Draft your pattern (see Sources: *The Magical Effects of Color*). Begin collecting fabrics for your design. When you are ready to begin your quilt, start in the design area which appears most comfortable. Work spontaneously.

57A. *My Spring Vignettes*, 1993, 59" x 54½"
Lynn Underwood, Saskatoon, Saskatchewan, Canada

Inspired by a class taught by Laurie Sobie, and Pepper Cory's book *Crosspatch*, Lynn explored the ideas of combining blocks while blending colors. Combining Shoofly with a star block, Lynn created an interesting blend of pattern and coloration. Photo: Courtesy of the artist

57B. *Red Hot Chili Peppers*, 1995, 45" x 45"
Sylvia Kundrats, Quakertown, Pennsylvania

This unique challenge wallhanging is Sylvia's first attempt at incorporating black and white into a design. Using two blocks, she attempted to use color to suggest the taste of red hot chili peppers. This is an original design using traditional blocks with variations. See page 46 for more details about this quilt. Photo: Ken Wagner

58A. *Tennessee Waltz*, 1994, 91" x 102"

Diane Ebner, Phoenix, Arizona

This Tennessee Waltz quilt uses Fifty-four-Forty or Fight and
Snowball patterns to create its design. Diane made this quilt after
being inspired by a quilt seen in *Scrap Quilts* by Judy Martin. Note the
subtle differences between this quilt and *Stars of Seabeck* (photo 74B),
which also used Fifty-four-Forty or Fight as its main block design.
Photo: Ken Wagner

CHAPTER FOUR

Wonder Blocks with Moving Parts

As a beginning quilter I never analyzed the worthiness of the block patterns I chose. As I continued making quilts, I could see some designs worked better than others. Some of my early disappointing experiences allowed me to see that a pattern may be enhanced with a little help from a pencil or eraser. Eventually I realized a pattern could be changed even for fun—just to create new design possibilities. This chapter presents ideas for changing a block's internal parts to add interest or beauty, or to explore intriguing design possibilities. A few suggestions are extraordinarily simple, yet they can be significantly effective. Others involve a bit more challenge. Ideas presented in this chapter include adding lines, de-emphasizing pattern pieces, eliminating lines, removing block sections, and rotating block parts.

Adding Design Lines

Many traditional blocks have one pattern piece or area that is out of proportion—it is too large to work well with the other pattern pieces. This is visually distracting. A pattern can be enhanced if the overly large piece is broken up. Both Star of Many Points and Tulip Lady Finger have large center areas (Figures 4-1A and 4-2A). The latter pattern has other large unattractive areas, too. Perhaps these large areas can be enhanced by wise fabric use. More than likely, the best course of action is to divide the large areas further by adding design lines. These create additional shapes. In Figures 4-1B and 4-2B lines have been added to create smaller pieces and increase

visual interest. Still, Tulip Lady Finger has large side pieces that could be divided further. Texture or print fabric would help give visual relief, while solid-colored fabric would accentuate the large space. The Tulip Lady Finger Variation, shown in Figure 4-2B, would be best used as a center block in a small medallion design.

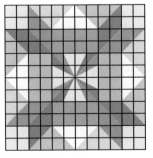

FIGURE 4-1A

The Star of Many Points (left) has a weak central focus. There is too much open space.

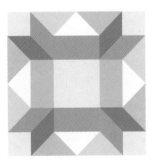
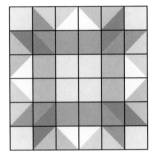

FIGURE 4-1B

To increase pattern interest, design lines have been added to the center area of Star of Many Points (nine-patch pattern: 12 x 12 = 144 square grid).

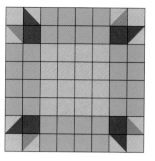
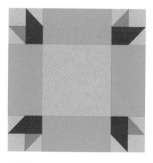

FIGURE 4-2A

Tulip Lady Finger has large spaces, which lack interest (left). Additional lines must be added to break up the design and create interest.

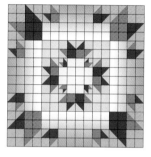

FIGURE 4-2B

This variation is an example of what might be done to enhance Tulip Lady Finger (four patch pattern: 16 x 16 = 256 square grid). (Variation: © Joen Wolfrom 1996)

Many traditional patterns have large background corner pieces, which appear fine when the block is viewed by itself. However, when multiple blocks are used, these corner spaces can be too large. If the background is too pronounced, so it competes visually with the foreground design, changes should be considered. One appealing way to handle large background areas is to use a wide variety of fabrics, subtly breaking up the background space. This can bring color and value changes that create a play of highlights and shadows in the background. If this doesn't appeal to you, or your fabric collection will not accommodate this idea, your best option is to break up the corner pieces.

Many isolated designs, like the Nine-Patch Star, have large background corners which are brought together in a traditional setting (Figures 4-3A and B). Adding two design lines in each corner piece makes three new pattern pieces appear (Figure 4-3C). This simple design change creates a new star dimension when the wider middle section abuts the star corners. Lines radiate like flower petals from behind the star (Figure 4-3D). When the block is placed in a quilt setting, the design appears much more delicate and organic than the original pattern. This simple change has resulted in a new pattern being formed—Star Flower (Figure 4-3E).

FIGURE 4-3A

Many patterns, such as Nine-Patch Star, have large background corner squares.

FIGURE 4-3B

When Nine-Patch Star blocks are put together, the four adjoining corners are accentuated, thus consuming much of the visual attention. This leads to the background space competing with the star design.

FIGURE 4-3C

Two design lines have been added to the corner squares of the Nine-Patch Star pattern. By doing this, three new pattern pieces have been created.

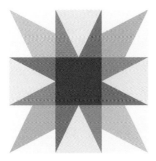

FIGURE 4-3D

These new corner design lines create the effect of a star being placed on petals. Because the design has changed considerably, a new pattern has evolved: Star Flower (nine-patch pattern: 6 x 6 = 36 square grid). (© Joen Wolfrom 1996)

FIGURE 4-3E

Star Flower has a gentler visual appearance than its parent the Nine-Patch Star. This new design creates more interest.

Sometimes an already successful block can be enhanced with small design changes. These additions rarely make the block unrecognizable. Instead, a pattern variation is conceived. For instance, I am particularly fond of the block Barbara Bannister's Star (Figure 4-4A). I felt the illusion of transparency could be promoted if I created a new shape at the places where overlapping occurred. So I added lines there. This changed version, which accentuates transparency, is named Barbara Bannister's Transparent Star (Figure 4-4B). An overall view can be seen on page 31 (Figure 2-7B).

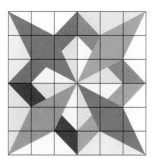

FIGURE 4-4A

Barbara Bannister's Star is a visually successful traditional pattern (nine-patch pattern: 6 x 6 = 36 square grid).

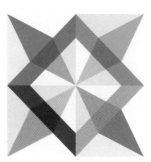

FIGURE 4-4B

By adding a few well-directed lines to Barbara Bannister's Star, transparency can be created. The result is Barbara Bannister's Transparent Star. (Variation by Joen Wolfrom 1991)

De-emphasizing Pattern Pieces

De-emphasizing pattern parts is a form of color and value play. It allows you to place a pattern piece visually into the background instead of keeping it in the foreground. This creates interesting illusions. Visual echoes may be created, sometimes appearing to dance far into the distance. The Nine-Patch Star (Figure 4-5A) is an easy design with which to work. Muting colors makes three star points appear to recede into the distance—they have been de-emphasized (Figure 4-5B). When these blocks are set together a subtle curved effect appears. De-emphasizing these star points diminishes the Nine-Patch Star's static effect (Figure 4-5C).

Many traditional patterns can be enhanced by de-emphasizing parts of the pattern, and subtle illusionary effects are created. To create this effect, you should use lighter valued and more toned (grayer) fabrics. Beth Gilbert's *Bethany Beach* uses de-emphasizing to create its design (photo 14B). Paul Schutte's *Declining Pineapple* uses de-emphasizing in his overall design (photo 70A). The result is a fascinating design with illusions of depth and transparency. Junko Sawada also uses de-emphasizing to increase her quilts' interest and beauty (photo 9A and 40B). Dorle Stern-Straeter has de-emphasized parts of her stars in *Starlit Night* (photo 16B). Likewise, *Night Flight Over a City* by Jean Liittschwager (photo 77A) and *Circles II* and *Circles III* by Reynola Pakusich (photos 84B and C) show examples of de-emphasizing pattern parts. Martie Huston's *Oblique Illusion* (photo 41A) creates a stunning three-dimensional illusion by de-emphasizing the foreground pattern in Jack's Chain.

FIGURE 4-5C
Here the Nine-Patch Star creates added interest with de-emphasized star points in a multi-block setting. It almost appears as if the star points are dancing.

Eliminating Pattern Pieces

Pattern pieces may be eliminated for several reasons. Perhaps the block appears too busy. Maybe there isn't enough open space in the pattern. If you feel a block is too complex, busy, or crowded, feel free to eliminate lines and pattern pieces. Sometimes you may want to change one or two lines just to give more flexibility to the design. Or you may want to explore design possibilities, as Anita Krug did in *Falling Into Place* (photo 101A).

The Nine-Patch Star is a simple pattern with which to experiment with pattern-piece elimination. If two star points are eliminated, the pattern makes a personality change (Figure 4-6A). It becomes quite contemporary in a quilt setting (Figure 4-6B). Different color application will give subtle changes (Figure 4-6C and D).

FIGURE 4-6A
To create more interest, you may eliminate certain parts of your pattern. Here the Nine-Patch Star has two star points eliminated.

FIGURE 4-5A
Nine-Patch Star (nine-patch pattern: 6 x 6 = 36 square grid)

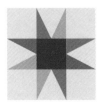

FIGURE 4-5B
You can add interest to the Nine-Patch Star by de-emphasizing some star points.

FIGURE 4-6B
By eliminating star points in this multi-block setting of Nine-Patch Star, a contemporary effect is created.

FIGURE 4-6C

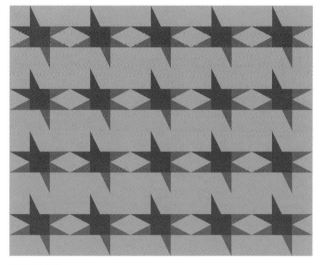

FIGURE 4-6D

Color and value changes can create added interest in a simple design.

Dorle Stern-Straeter eliminated star points in *Starlit Night* (photo 16B). This creates a feeling of movement from star to star. Anita Krug eliminated a few window panes in *Something Fishy* (photo 117C), giving the design open areas. Consequently, Anita has enhanced her design by creating variation, thus avoiding too much repetition. Emilie Belak created design attention by eliminating the upper part of her triangular pattern and replacing it with flying birds (photo 15A). This was a very innotative substitution. In *Winter Nights—A Candle Burns* (photo 73A) Kaye Rhodes has eliminated several pattern pieces as the design moves from the center area to the quilt's outer perimeter. Because our eyes like intricacy, we automatically focus on the more complicated design area. This focus is enhanced further by Kaye's color plan.

Once lines have been erased, blocks can be copied and put together in a paper-play fashion. You can quickly judge the success of the design. Is it dynamic? Are some parts interesting and others not? Do you need to make more changes? Does the block respond well to your erasings? Was the block a poor choice? Should you se-

lect another block? Once you have played with a few designs, make observations about what you like and don't like. When you are excited about one particular design, make tentative color and fabric plans. Consider what illusions, if any, you may wish to incorporate. When you are ready to begin, draft the pattern in your favorite method. (See *The Magical Effects of Color*, Appendix II, pages 120-122, for patch-pattern drafting instructions.)

Removing a Section of the Block Pattern

With certain blocks you can develop interesting designs by eliminating portions of the pattern. Ordinarily, identical blocks placed together have a mirror image effect on each other. The pattern pieces in each block's outer sections are arranged with a reversal of right and left, as if one was reflecting the other in a mirror. You can see this with Barbara Bannister's Transparent Star (Figure 4-7A and B).

FIGURE 4-7A

Most traditional patterns are mirror-image designs.

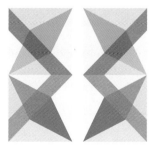

FIGURE 4-7B

The adjacent pattern pieces in each block are arranged with a reversal of right and left as if one is reflecting the other in a mirror.

Some blocks, however, have no mirror image reflection when placed together. Instead, these blocks have identical sides. The traditional four-patch Storm at Sea pattern has this repeating characteristic (Figure 4-8A). Its traditional quilt setting is shown in Figure 4-8B. This popular pattern creates a sea of fabric waves with illusionary curves. For a slightly different effect, consider taking out one of the vertical repeating sections, thereby forcing adjacent blocks to share the common outer portion (Figure 4-8C). As you can see in Figure 4-8D, the overall design changes subtly when this is done. Going further, all repeating sections can be eliminated, so that blocks share common sides both horizontally and vertically (Figure 4-8E). When this is done the overall pattern changes even more. In this Storm at Sea variation stars become visible as the four block sections come together (Figure 4-8F). This block change can be very effective. Maureen McGee and Sarah Dickson's Storm at Sea quilt, along with Mary Gillis' *Call Me, Moby,* were created by removing these repetitive block parts (photos 69A and B).

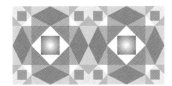

FIGURE 4-8A

Storm at Sea's outer sections create repetitive patterning when placed side by side.

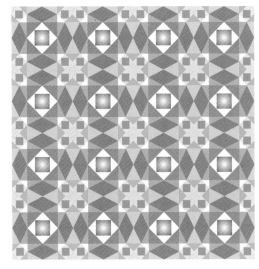

FIGURE 4-8B

The traditional setting of Storm at Sea is shown here.

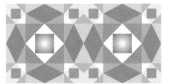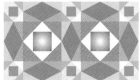

FIGURE 4-8C

One block's repetitious vertical section can be eliminated. Thus an outside section is shared by adjoining blocks.

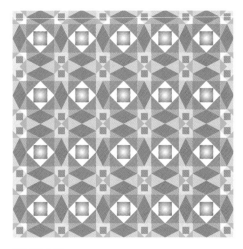

FIGURE 4-8D

In this variation, blocks share adjacent outer vertical portions.

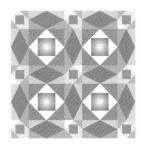

FIGURE 4-8E

Another variation can be created by having the blocks share both the vertical and horizontal outer block portions. A star becomes pronounced.

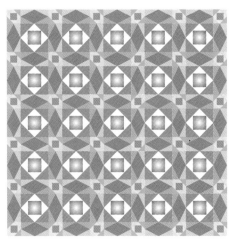

FIGURE 4-8F

When repetitive sections are eliminated, a star is emphasized.

REVERSING THE ACTION— ADDING MORE REPETITIONS

With a pattern that creates design repetitions such as the Storm at Sea, the repetitions can be accentuated. Instead of taking out extra sections, more can be added (Figure 4-9A). Further echoing is created with the repetitive patterning (Figure 4-9B) This effect can be enhanced by working with a multitude of fabrics.

FIGURE 4-9A

By placing a repeated pattern section between blocks, greater echoing is created.

FIGURE 4-9B

Rotating Block Parts

For additional block interest, you may want to explore the idea of rotating one or more sections of your block's pattern. Sometimes this is done to eliminate an overly static design. In addition, rotating portions of blocks can be used to make unexpected, wonderful new designs. A block does not have to be complicated to be successful.

Star Flower, the new design created by adding lines to the Nine-Patch Star, has four square corner designs that can be rotated (Figure 4-10A). Another new pattern is created by rotating these square corners 180 degrees (Figure 4-10B). In a quilt setting, such as that shown in Figures 4-10C, this new design looks quite different from both the Nine-Patch Star and its relative, Star

Flower (Figure 4-10A). It has been given the name Dancing Star because the stars appear to dance when placed in a multiple-block setting. With a subtle color change the design shifts its overall focus. This can be seen in Figures 4-10D and E.

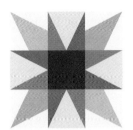

FIGURE 4-10A

FIGURE 4-10B

By placing the wide part of the corner squares outward, a subtle design change results.

FIGURE 4-10C

Star Flower patterns differ because their corner squares are placed in opposing positions.

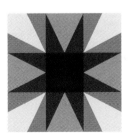

FIGURE 4-10D

With a subtle color change, the Nine-Patch Star can change its focus yet again.

FIGURE 4-10E

By accentuating the large triangular shapes between star points, the star's lattice design is formed in this version of Dancing Star.

Arlene Stamper rotated the North Carolina Lily blocks in *Koinonia Garden* (photo 11A). This setting is much more interesting than if she had placed the blocks in the usual traditional block setting. Kay Lettau's *Trail to Tranquility* has been rotated into a dynamic asymmetrical design (photo 76A).

Junko Sawada's *Bird's Song* incorporates many innovative design changes (photo 10A). She has divided her block into parts and rotated these throughout her quilt. Also, to enhance the impression of freedom, Junko has rotated whole blocks.

Another exciting quilt has been created by Debby Baum, who has taken several steps to create her free-flowing design *Fall's Folly* (photo 80C). She broke apart the leaf pattern, dividing it into four one-leaf quadrants. Then she rotated these quadrants throughout the quilt, allowing the leaves to fall spontaneously. In addition, she staggered the partial blocks to allow for more flexibility.

Blocks with circular designs give wonderful visual play to the design. New York Beauty is a great quilt block with which to explore the concept of rotation. Reynola Pakusich has created a wonderful quilt by rotating this pattern (photo 70B).

Most patch patterns have design sections that can be rotated to add interest, flexibility, or challenge. There are no rules for rotating block parts. It's purely what pleases you that counts. It is exciting to see the evolution of a new design take place.

Creative Block Changes: A Jumping-Off Point

Sometimes a particular block inspires my creative juices. When I look at the block, my mind begins to see different ways I could change the design. The traditional block becomes my jumping-off point—a place to begin my creative adventure. With some blocks a flash of an idea comes immediately: I know exactly how I am going to change it. At other times I play with the design slowly: changing, moving, adding, or removing existing lines or design elements. I work until I create something I like, or until I give up in muddled scribbles, which have gone nowhere.

I liked the pattern Century of Progress (Figure 4-11), but I didn't want to deal with the uneven diagonal squares, so I began playing with ideas. My first experimentation resulted in the block Floating Jacks (Figures 2-9A and B, page 32). Further exploration led to a completely different design. This block play resulted in Glowing Stars and Gems (Figures 4-12A and B). Even though the two blocks appear to have little in common, the diagonal squares stepping into the corners intrigued me. I wanted the blocks to flow into each other. Also, I wanted to create a pattern that could incorporate depth, luminosity, luster, and transparency when placed in a multiple-block setting. Another person may use the same Century of Progress pattern as a jumping-off point, but end up with a completely different design. Inspiration does not follow the same path for any two people. Take time to create your own traditional block patterns. It's great fun!

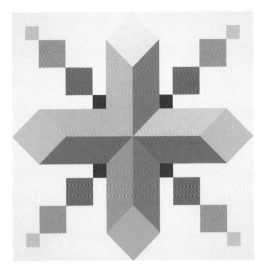

FIGURE 4-11

Century of Progress was the block inspiration used to create both original blocks: Floating Jacks and Glowing Stars and Gems.

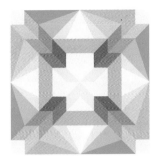 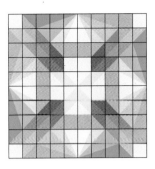

FIGURE 4-12A

Glowing Stars and Gems is an original block pattern, which was inspired by the Century of Progress block. Even though the two blocks appear to have little in common, the diagonal squares stepping into the corners intrigued me. After playing with numerous ideas, this block was created. This five-patch pattern is one of my favorite original designs. (10 x 10 = 100 square grid) (© Joen Wolfrom 1991)

FIGURE 4-12B

I wanted the blocks to flow into each other. Also, I wanted to create many design options with which to work. Therefore, depth, luminosity, luster, and transparency can all be created with this overall pattern.

Activities and Extended Learning

1. Choose a simple patch pattern. Change the pattern by adding lines to it. These line additions should increase the number of shapes in the pattern. When finished, make copies of your block variation. Paste the blocks together into a paper quilt. Do you like the design? If so, consider making a small quilt using this design. If you are not pleased with your changes, evaluate what needs to be done. Begin working with the block again. When you are satisfied, make more copies. Put these blocks together into a paper quilt. Reassess.

2. Select another pattern with which to work. After studying the pattern, decide which shapes you would like to de-emphasize or eliminate from the design. Use white-out to eliminate lines. Color your pattern. Show how your pattern has changed through de-emphasizing by changing the color values in your pattern pieces.

3. Using Storm at Sea (four-patch pattern) or another pattern with repetitious outer sections, make fifteen to twenty-five copies of the block. Investigate different ways you can create design variations. You may choose to create quilt designs similar to the ones shown in this chapter; however, attempt to investigate further. Consider creating variations by combining the different suggestions into one quilt design. If you like the design you have created, make a quilt using your drawing as a guide.

4. Choose a block in which to rotate one or more sections. It may be easiest if you choose a block that can be divided easily into quadrants (one-fourth sections). Make several copies of the block. Cut the blocks apart in their quadrant sections. Begin putting the blocks back together by rotating the different sections. Do not feel you must work in a repetitive manner. Your pattern may dictate a spontaneous rotation plan. Do what seems best to you. If you want, make several quilt settings. In one, rotate all the blocks systematically. Do another, again rotating the blocks systematically, but choose another manner of rotation. Lastly, create a more spontaneous design by rotating the block sections haphazardly.

5. Choose a block that has elements that both please and displease you. Draw the block, putting in only the lines and shapes that appeal to you. Leave out those that displease you. Begin adding lines and shapes, thereby creating a new design. Make several copies of the block after you have finished your drawing, and make a paper quilt. Study your quilt design. If there are any areas that need changing, figure out what must be done. Consider creating this quilt as a future project.

69A. *Storm at Sea,* 1988, 86" x 96"
Maureen McGee, Lansing, Kansas, and
Sarah A. Dickson, San Antonio, Texas

Maureen and Sarah have created a fascinating
design using the Storm at Sea pattern. Notice
they have eliminated all repetitious side sections
of adjoining blocks. Doing this accentuates a
nine-patch star design. Photo: Ken Wagner

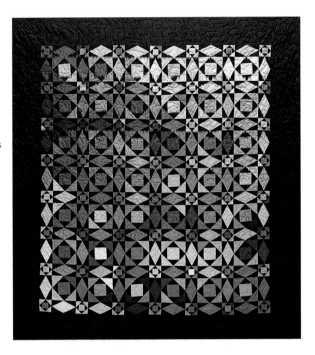

69B. *Call me Moby,* 1994, 48" x 48"
Mary L. Gillis, Boston, Massachusetts

Mary is fascinated with the illusion of curves in designs like Storm
at Sea. This quilt was a chance for Mary to pay homage to her
favorite book, *Moby Dick,* and a favorite quilt pattern. Mary's quilt
was inspired by one created by Susan Varanka of Meriden, Connecticut, whose quilt was shown on the back cover of *Quilter's Newsletter
Magazine.* Mary eliminated all repetitious side sections of adjoining
blocks, thus creating a pronounced star design. Hand quilted by
Genevieve Berumen, Cambridge, Massachusetts. Photo: Ken Wagner

70A. *Declining Pineapple*, 1994, 80" x 80"
Paul Schutte, Potchefstroom, South Africa

Using the traditional Pineapple Log Cabin pattern, Paul has created a most tantalizing design. By unique placement of the colors and values throughout the design surface, portions of the pattern have been diminished, creating a play of depth and transparency. Private collection of Rick and Margie Garratt. Photo: Photographic Services, University of Potchefstroom, South Africa

70B. *Contemporary New York Beauty*, 1994, 41" x 50"
Reynola Pakusich, Bellingham, Washington

Reynola created the path and circles in this design by dividing her different blocks into sections. She never anticipated the mathematical dilemma she was creating as the partial circles moved around the design surface. So it became quite a challenge to arrange this beautiful design. Reynola enjoyed using a variety of ethnic and hand-designed fabrics, including batik, air-brushed, Japanese Ikat, and Indonesian Ikat. She was inspired by Judy Pollard's paper foundation technique and Karen Stone's New York Beauty quilt. Photo: Ken Wagner

71A. *Through the Gazebo Window*, 1985, 62" x 86"
Caryl Bryer Fallert, Oswego, Illinois

Caryl created a fabric landscape with a very literal, three-dimensional foreground fading into a more abstract background. This landscape became a composite of Caryl's favorite springtime images. She strip-pieced two-inch strips of different print and solid fabrics, using more than three hundred fabrics. The composition was drawn full size on bristol board and pinned to her studio wall. The garden scene within the window is divided into a series of rhomboid-shaped blocks. Photo: Courtesy of the artist

72A and 72B. *Two Minutes in May,* 1995, 78" x 41"
Shirley P. Kelly, Colden, New York

72B Back

This spectacular quilt is both dramatic and intriguing. Originally, both sides of this quilt were worked out from photographs as demos for Shirley's high school art students. She transferred this activity to her own quiltmaking, creating two separate quilts which are related. The classic horse race is filled with energy and suspense. The quilt's back is charming with its foal prancing toward the rosebush. The rosebush and foal are hand appliquéd. The Star of the Bluegrass blocks are pieced by machine and then hand appliquéd in position. Photo: Ken Wagner

73A. *Winter Nights—A Candle Burns*, 1989, 32" x 36"
Kaye E. Rhodes, Annandale, Virginia

The Arrowhead Star block that had been used for Kaye's guild's wallhanging challenge had to be simplified as she made progress on the design. Each center area block was made from thirty pieces. However, the block changed subtly as it moved outward, due to fabric and time constraints. The dark blocks along the perimeter are made from eighteen pieces. Arrowhead Star was designed by Jinny Beyer, and is included in her book *Quilter's Album of Blocks and Borders*. Photo: Lloyd Wolf, Arlington, Virginia

73B. *Kaye-oss,* 1995, 55" x 42"
Kaye E. Rhodes, Annandale, Virginia

Kaye-oss is the result of the transformation of the hexagon to equilateral triangles and sixty-degree diamonds, thus actually combining related traditional patterns. In addition, the value placement creates dimension from one configuration to the next. Kaye used Pandora's Box of Quick Strip™ templates to rotary cut and machine piece the design. Photo: Ken Wagner

74A. *Rotating Stars for Africa*, 1990, 78" x 90"
Paul Schutte, Potchefstroom, South Africa

Using the traditional Pinwheel pattern, Paul has created stars which look as if they are rotating in space. Changing the colors and values makes the design much more dynamic than the traditional Pinwheel block setting. Photo: Photographic Services, University of Potchefstroom, South Africa

74B. *Stars of Seabeck*, 1995, 96" x 96"
Sue Williams, Gig Harbor, Washington

This beautiful quilt is a variation of the traditional pattern Fifty-four-Forty or Fight. Sue combined this block with an elongated triangle to create the graceful illusionary curves. The outer portion of this quilt has been hand stippled; no two lines ever intersect. Photo: Ken Wagner

75A. *Lafayette Square*, 1993, 62" x 37"
The Tuesday Quilters

This wonderful group quilt was created by quilters who combined their talents quite successfully. Appliqué, piecing, machine embroidery, and painting were used. See page 120 for further details. Collection of Shirley Banks. Photo: Mark Gulezian

From left to right, the panels were made by: Kathryn Vitek, Rockville, Maryland; Verena Levine, Washington, D.C.; Lee Porter, Washington, D.C.; Lauren Kingsland, Gaithersburg, Maryland; Donna Radner, Chevy Chase, Maryland; Amy Frank Lindberg, Hays, Kansas; Carol Clanton, Aurora, Colorado; Ann Hoenigswald, Washington, D.C.; and Lynne Bradley, Takoma Park, Maryland.

75B. *Georgetown on the Potomac*, 1995, 68" x 43", The Tuesday Quilters

This contemporary friendship quilt was created by several members of The Tuesday Quilters and friends. The design is an interpretation of a photograph chosen by the group. The quilt is pieced, appliquéd, machine and hand embroidered, and has button trim. For further details, see page 120. Photo: Mark Gulezian

From left to right, the panels were made by: Sarah Sagalow, Germantown, Maryland; Verena Levine, Washington, D.C.; Kathryn Vitek, Rockville, Maryland; Carla Bonifasi, Scottsdale, Arizona; Michelle Gilchrist, Phoenix, Arizona; Lauren Kingsland, Gaithersburg, Maryland; Amy Frank Lindberg, Hays, Kansas; Lee Porter, Washington, D.C.; and Gertrude Braan, Washington, D.C.

76A. *Trail to Tranquility*, 1994, 70" x 70"
Kay Lettau, Annandale, Virginia

Kay was inspired by an antique scrap quilt made from the traditional
block Snake in a Hollow. The original quilt was made in pastels with a
traditional straight set. Using her own dynamic coloration, Kay's design
interpretation is very innovative. The quilt contains many Japanese
fabrics. The quilting design is Sashiko. Exquisitely hand-quilted by Gayle
Ropp, New York City. Photo: Ken Wagner

76B. *Friends All Around*, 1994, 62" x 62"
Ellen Anderson, Flagstaff, Arizona

Friends All Around creates continual interest with its color play,
block-size variation, and overall design. Movement, transparency,
and depth have all been achieved through fabric use and color
placement. Photo: Ken Wagner

77A. *Night Flight Over a City,* 1988, 57" x 72"
Jean Liittschwager, Leaburg, Oregon

Using an adaptation of the traditional Geese in the Pond pattern, this quilt was inspired by the many flights Jean has enjoyed with her husband in a small airplane. The quilting was designed to show the wind generated by the aircraft. Photo: Jean Liittschwager

77B. *Afterglow,* 1995, 56" x 56"
Lynda Kelley, Tacoma, Washington

Lynda used the Nine-Patch Square pattern to create her foreground's woven pattern. In addition, she graduated the background colors to create further interest. Depth and a sense of a light source has been achieved. Photo: Ken Wagner

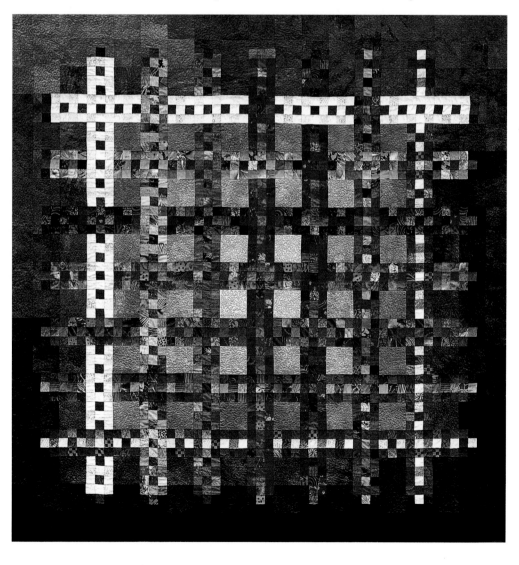

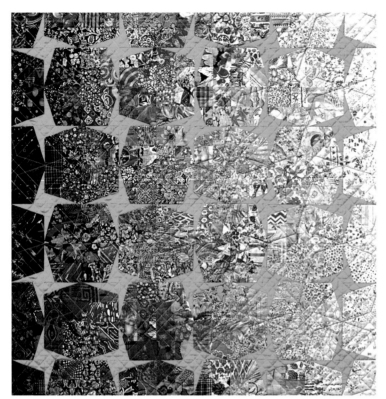

78A. *Colourwash and Blue Windmills,* 1996, 36" x 36"
Deirdre Amsden, London, England

The innovator of colourwash quilts, Deirdre continues to explore ways to create three-dimensionality on a two-dimensional surface. Deirdre, a leading international quilt artist, is able to combine a wide assortment of fabrics to make the most spectacular colourwash artworks. One such example of Deirdre's exploration is *Colourwash and Blue Windmills.* Photo: James Austin

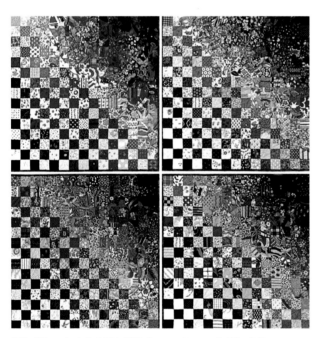

78B. *Colouration 1, 2, 3 & 4,* 1992, four sections each 24" x 24"
Deirdre Amsden, London, England

Colouration 1, 2, 3, & 4 are four related pieces which may be hung in many different arrangements. The checkerboard pattern visually connects the four sections while the coloring changes from achromatic to polychromatic. Photo: Andrea Heselton

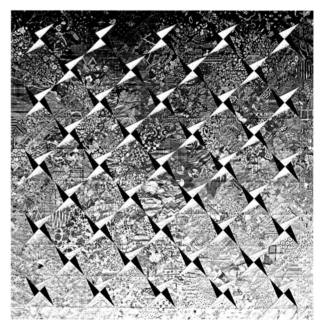

78C. *Colourwash Windmill Grid II,* 1996, 44" x 44"
Deirdre Amsden, London, England

Deirdre is masterful at blending fabrics, colors, and values together to create fascinating illusions. *Colourwash Windmill Grid II* is another example of intriguing design, exquisite workmanship, and superb fabric and color blending. Photo: James Austin

79A. *Sandscape*, 1990, 63" x 63"
Dorle Stern-Straeter, München, Germany

Dorle, a noted international quilt artist, designed a kite-shaped block for this quilt. She then divided this block into a nine-patch. She divided alternating block corners into two triangles. In this way she created pyramids. To create the overall design she tessellated her blocks. This quilt is rich in design and color. Photo: Wolfgang Zuppée

79B. *No Exit*, 1994, 65" x 64"
Dorle Stern-Straeter, München, Germany

Dorle has experimented and developed her own intricate technique to create her quilt art. In *No Exit* she uses a kite-shaped block to begin her design. By breaking the block further and shading the colors from dark to light, she creates another innovative design. Photo: Patricia Fliegauf

80A. *Breaking Free*, 1994, 53" x 53"
Gloria Hansen, Hightstown, New Jersey

The base block from *Breaking Free* was inspired by Gloria's earlier quilt *Awakenings* (photo 12A). This take-off on the block was designed on a Macintosh computer using Canvas 3.5. Many fabrics used are ones Gloria either painted, airbrushed, or dyed. Photo: Courtesy of the artist

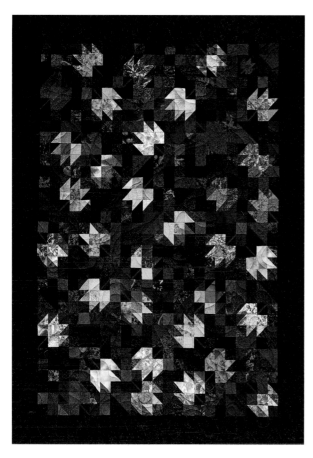

80B. *Friendly Challenge*, 1994, 24½" x 57½"
Peggy Hill, Ithaca, New York; Connie Tenpas, Clymer, New York; Barbara Godfrey, Oakville, Ontario, Canada

In this sampler challenge quilt each participant used a common fabric for her block. Traditional blocks were Castle Cross (Peggy's) and Drunkard's Path (Connie's). Barbara's block is an original design. The quilt was set and quilted by Peggy. Appliqué used in setting half-squares was a modification of an Elly Sienkiewicz Baltimore Album block. Photo: Ken Wagner

80C. *Fall's Folly,* 1994, 59" x 79"
Debra Baum, Traverse City, Michigan

This spirited quilt was made using the traditional Maple Leaf pattern. Debra wanted her quilt to reflect the dark patchy forest floor of northern Michigan in October with all the beautifully colored, newly-fallen autumn leaves strewn and scattered by the wind. She used a collection of dark, muted, low-contrasting fabrics for the background, while the leaves' fabrics were made from bright, highly contrasting fabric. This quilt was inspired by Lynne Stewart's (Mansfield, Massachusetts) *Enchanted Maple*. Photo: Ken Wagner.

81A. *Autumn Praise,* 1995, 76" x 76"
Carol Webb, Tulsa, Oklahoma

This Maple Leaf quilt is the second in a series made by Carol.
In this quilt she has shifted the background colors to create
a sense of light play, adding further interest to the design.
Photo: Ken Wagner

81B. *Rahr-West Mansion Panels,* 1994, 56" x 51"
The Ladies of the Lake of Manitowoc County, Wisconsin

Phyllis Krueger, Sally Kahlenberg, Brenda DeBruyn, Claire
Amato, Judy LaGrow, Jean Lowden, Lucy Zeldenrust,
Shirley Suettinger

This friendship quilt, created by The Ladies of the Lake,
was a challenge to the group prompted by the urging of
Shirley Suettinger. Each panel is 7" x 51". Although they
were not certain they could handle the intricate project, it
was an overwhelming success. For further details, see page
118. Photo: Ken Wagner

82A. *Star Check: The Quilted Generation*, 1994, 74" x 89"
Wendy Richardson, Brooklyn Park, Minnesota

Wendy's fascination with color movement within a quilt's surface inspires her to create wonderfully innovative quilts based on traditional patterns. Besides playing with color, Wendy has allowed her foreground pattern to stretch, bringing increased interest to the surface design in *Star Check: The Quilted Generation*. Photo: Ken Wagner

82B. *Gaslamp Quarter*, 1995, 70" x 68"
Margaret J. Miller, Woodinville, Washington

Margaret's *Gaslamp Quarter* was developed as part of her investigation to find various ways to move color values across a pieced surface with half-square and half-rectangle triangles. This quilt is just one of numerous innovative quilts created by Margaret. For further investigation and exciting examples of quilt exploration, study Margaret's books (see Sources). Photo: Courtesy of That Patchwork Place

83A. *Building Memories*, 1995, 48" x 48"
Helen Courtice, Penticton, British Columbia, Canada

Helen created this innovative quilt from the traditional pattern Memory. It began as an experiment while Helen was drafting squares into diamonds. Her first intention had been to arrange these diamonds into a star shape. Displeased with the result, she persisted with design play until the cube arrangement evolved. The value shading followed quickly when Helen realized she had created a three-dimensional effect. Photo: Marianne Parsons

83B. *Autumn Perspective*, 1984, 60" x 72"
Caryl Bryer Fallert, Oswego, Illinois

Caryl wanted to create a grid of three-dimensional windows with an abstract landscape behind them. Since autumn colors are her personal favorites, she chose a fall landscape. She created the feeling of looking out at a forest in autumn without being able to discern any specific object. Some windows are quilted in leaf patterns; the brown window grid is quilted in a free-form wood grain pattern. (To order Caryl's new book, see Sources.) Photo: Courtesy of the artist

84A. *Introspection*, 1995, 53" x 68"
Jennie Peck, Alexander, New York

Jennie drew her own original block, which she named Offset Frame. With this pattern she created a very contemporary design by having the blocks seem to float above the background. Her exquisite background coloring was achieved by well-placed use of pointillist fabric. Depth, luminosity, and transparency are evident. Photo: Courtesy of the artist

84B. *Circles II*, 1995, 45" x 45"
Reynola Pakusich, Bellingham, Washington

Reynola used the background of cut-out circles from a previous quilt and matched the color, darkening the value for the background squares of this quilt. Then she organized the value flow across the quilt. Reynola used a variety of ethnic and hand-designed fabrics including Fl-Air air-brushed and marbled fabrics. Photo: Ken Wagner

84C. *Circles III,* 1995, 30" x 30"
Reynola Pakusich, Bellingham, Washington

Again Reynola used the background of cut-out circles from a previous quilt to create *Circles III*. In this quilt she lightened the value of each background square before organizing the value flow. She let the value increase flow into the border. Photo: Ken Wagner

85A. *In Praise of Poppies,* 1994, 48" x 56"

Emilie Belak, Grand Forks, British Columbia, Canada

Emilie has made several wonderful quilts which celebrate our earth's beauty. Her beautiful garden with lovely flowers helps inspire her creativity. Each year the Oriental poppies usher in the summer season with their brilliant colors. So, Emilie wished to pay tribute to them by creating a poppy quilt. She combined numerous ideas and techniques to create this breathtaking three-dimensional art work. Photo: Carina Woolrich. Courtesy of Quilt San Diego

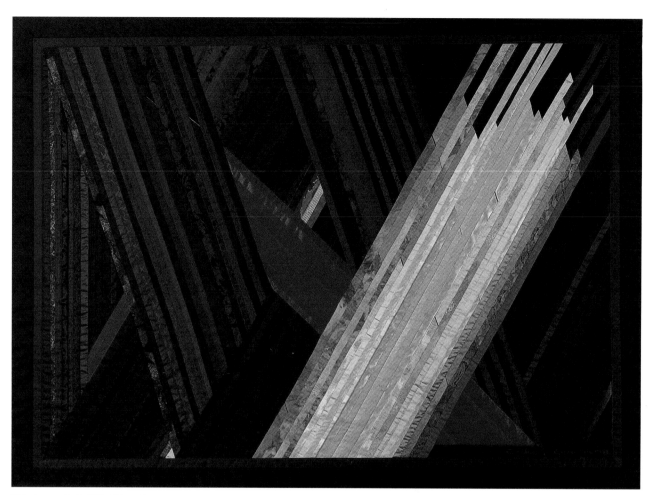

86A. *January Quilt,* 1993, 67" x 49"
Erika Odemer, München, Germany

Internationally renowned, Erika creates museum-quality works of
art using fabric as her medium. A signature of her creations is her
dramatic use of rich colors and strong design lines. One such
example is *January Quilt.* Here the magnificent hues are created by
using silk fabrics which have been dyed or over-dyed by Erika.
Photo: Patricia Fliegauf, München, Germany

CHAPTER FIVE

Making the Block Design More Flexible

In the previous chapter we examined several ways the basic block structure could be changed internally. In this chapter we explore ways to give the block external changes to promote new design opportunities. These ideas include rotating blocks, dropping blocks, varying the blocks' sizes, staggering blocks, floating blocks, and moving one block into another block's space. A few options are closely related; their differences are subtle. Combining any one of these ideas with your own personal flair should result in interesting outcomes

Rotating Blocks

When working with an asymmetrical block design, you may create more flexibility and interest if you rotate the blocks. This rotation can be a one-fourth, one-half, or three-fourths turn of a block, as seen in the Maple Leaf pattern (Figure 5-1A, B, C, and D). The result of rotating gives the quilt a feeling of freedom or spontaneity (Figure 5-1E). Janice Richard's *Tribute to Tippi Hedren* is a wonderful illustration of rotating blocks throughout the quilt's surface (photo 100C). Although this is not a traditional pattern, the manner in which Janice worked can be adapted to any asymmetrical traditional pattern. After Janice drew her block she made several small paper copies of it. Positioning the paper blocks identically resulted in too much rigidity, so she began rotating her blocks. As she did this, the idea of birds flying in the sky began to evolve. Janice decided to create a sunrise-to-sunset sky with her background fabrics. For more discussion about Janice's quilt see page 131.

In Junko Sawada's *Bird's Song,* blocks have been rotated in a spontaneous fashion (photo 10A). To create even more freedom of movement, Junko has rotated some of her blocks' internal parts too. Some lilies have changed direction within a single block.

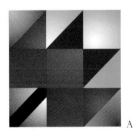 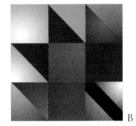

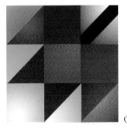 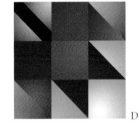

FIGURES 5-1A–D

The traditional pattern Maple Leaf can create an exciting asymmetrical design, if the blocks are rotated throughout the surface. Four possible rotating positions are shown here.

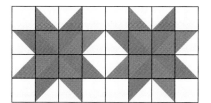

FIGURE 5-1E

By rotating the asymmetrical block Maple Leaf, you can create a unique quilt with continual movement. This example shows just one possibility with this pattern.

Dropping Blocks

One way to add interest in a quilt is to drop rows of blocks within the quilt setting. Static blocks or isolated patterns are especially enhanced by this setting. The design appears less rigid when the rows are allowed some movement. Four-patch blocks drop easily at the one-fourth, one-half, or three-fourths divisions (Figure 5-2). A nine-patch pattern can be dropped at the one-third, two-thirds, or even one-half divisions (Figure 5-3). A five-patch pattern can be dropped at any of its natural markings (Figure 5-4). Each position creates a slightly different overall design.

Generally blocks are positioned in straight vertical and horizontal rows, as seen in Figure 5-5A. The design appears less static when the block rows are dropped vertically. Dropping rows may be applied identically throughout the entire design, as in Figure 5-5B, where the rows are dropped in two-thirds intervals. For more variety the amount of dropping can vary between rows, as seen in Figure 5-5C. Consider varying the degree of dropping by being purposefully unpredictable. When

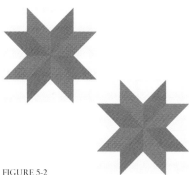

FIGURE 5-2

When using a rigidly-set four-patch pattern, like Evening Star, you can increase overall interest by dropping blocks. These dropped blocks can be positioned at their natural grid lines: one-fourth, one-half, or three-fourths markings.

the blocks are dropped, partial blocks must be placed at the top and bottom of some rows to conform to the quilt's edges. Custom-made blocks need to be made so they fit precisely in their selected places (Figure 5-5C).

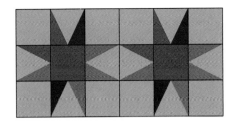

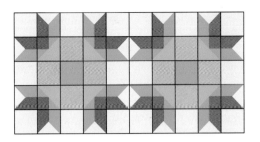

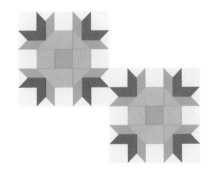

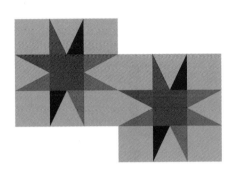

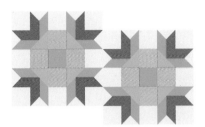

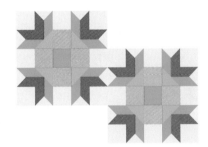

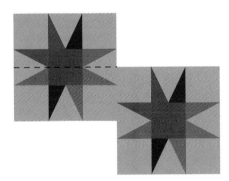

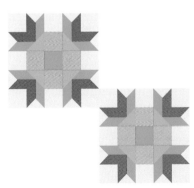

FIGURE 5-3

When using static nine-patch patterns, the design can be enhanced by dropping block rows. These can be dropped at their natural block divisions: one-third or two thirds grid lines. Also, you may use the one-half block division, if it can be easily established.

FIGURE 5-4

When dropping blocks in the five-patch pattern family, use the natural grid lines for positioning the blocks: one-fifth, two-fifths, three-fifths, or four-fifths. Does and Darts is used here as an example.

You may slide the blocks horizontally across the quilt surface, too. This horizontal shifting will add flexibility to your design. The idea and method remain the same; only the direction is different.

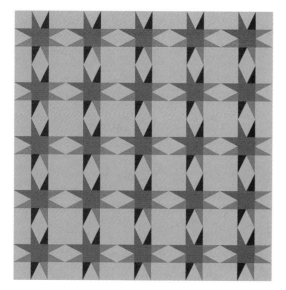

FIGURE 5-5A

Generally, blocks are positioned in straight vertical and horizontal rows, as shown here. Often this gives a static feeling with isolated patterns.

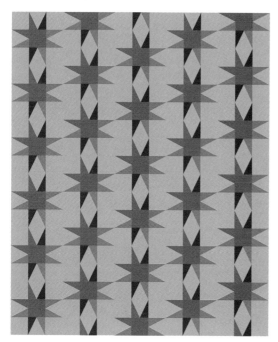

FIGURE 5-5B

Theses star rows are dropped in two-thirds intervals. The setting is more flexible than in the traditional setting. Partial blocks have been constructed and placed on the tops and bottoms of the rows, so that the edges are even.

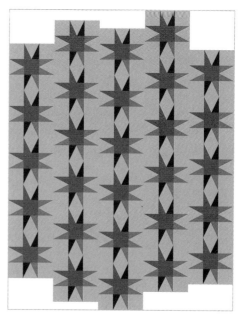

FIGURE 5-5C

In this setting, the rows are dropped randomly in unequal intervals. This gives the most flexible setting of the three samples shown here. Notice partial blocks must be made to fit into the rows' uneven tops and bottoms.

Varying Block Sizes

Changing the block size throughout the design presents a fun and interesting challenge, if you enjoy drafting and working with asymmetrical design. It is similar to working with a jigsaw puzzle. Choose a block with easy construction. Two methods for designing this type of quilt are discussed below, although many quiltmakers may choose to work without any plan.

METHOD ONE:
THE BASIC BLOCK DETERMINES THE QUILT SIZE

Select your block and determine its size. All other blocks will have a natural ratio to this basic block. For example, a twelve-inch Nine-Patch Star can have companion blocks, which are in two-inch increments. This results in two-, four-, six-, eight-, and ten-inch blocks (Figures 5-6A, B, C, D, and E). Or the blocks can be divisible by three, with three-, six-, and nine-inch blocks. Also, your blocks can be larger than the basic block, as long as the proportions are common to the basic block (e.g., 14, 16, 18, or 15, 18, 21; Figure 5-6F).

Once you have decided on the blocks' sizes, cut several miniature squares to represent these different blocks. Begin playing with your design. Since it may be difficult to fit the blocks together perfectly, *fillers* can be used to cover open background spaces. Fillers are small background areas that are not part of any block. These fillers can be any size or shape; however, they work best when their size and shape relate to the blocks' design. Work with the placement of your blocks until the entire quilt surface has been covered with blocks and fillers. Color, value, and fabric selection are used to create visual balance between the blocks.

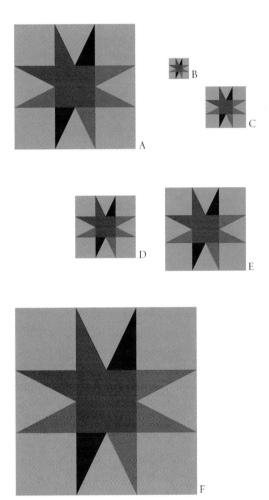

FIGURE 5-6A–F

A multi-sized block quilt may be created by using blocks with a dimensional relationship. If you start with a basic twelve-inch block (6A), other sizes could include two- (6B), four- (6C), six- (6D), and eight-inch blocks (6E). Larger blocks, such as an eighteen-inch block, could be used if they are divisible by two.

METHOD TWO:
THE QUILT SIZE DETERMINES THE BLOCKS' SIZES

For a more creative, challenging approach, draw your quilt's outline to scale on paper. If the proposed quilt is five feet by seven feet, draw a rectangle five inches by seven inches (or some other similar ratio; e.g., 10 x 14). Next, divide the quilt surface into random-sized squares and rectangles. Each square will represent one block. Fillers may also be used to help cover the background space. An in-progress design is shown in Figure 5-7. The stars can vary greatly in size throughout the quilt top. There are unlimited ways to arrange the blocks in the quilt surface.

FIGURE 5-7

A multi-sized block quilt may be created by fitting blocks into a designated area. Here blocks are placed randomly in a rectangular area. Blocks can be any size, as long as they fit into the total surface design. In this in-progress design, proposed fillers and spaces for more star blocks are shown in the non-colored areas.

If you have a representational (i.e., pictorial) design, consider using several rectangular blocks in the design, because they allow more freedom than square blocks. Rectangles can be placed either vertically or horizontally. Ellen Anderson has maneuvered the houses (and barn) around her quilt's surface very cleverly. Ellen alternates the houses with pieced "space" blocks in *Friends All Around* (photo 76B), allowing a feeling of openness and movement in this charming neighborhood.

THE BALANCING ACT

While planning your quilt's design, be aware of how well the shapes are balanced with each other. Play with your design until you are pleased with your efforts. If you plan to use a wide variety of fabrics in your quilt, be aware of how the block sizes, colors, and fabric selection will affect the visual balance of the overall design. Asymmetrical balance is achieved through distribution of visual weight. Both sides of the quilt's surface must either weigh the same visually, or they must be equally interesting. Both the visual weight and the eye-catching attraction are created through manipulating colors, shapes, sizes, values, and textures.

Contrasts in color help achieve asymmetrical balance. The largest block in your design may be overwhelming, so less attention-getting fabrics and colors must be chosen for it. If the largest block still attracts too much attention, try placing bright, colorful fabrics elsewhere to create a more balanced effect. Because our eyes are more interested in bright colors than in grayed-down colors, placing brightly-colored fabrics in several small areas can dilute the larger object's visual strength. As a result, our eyes are attracted to both areas of the design.

If you place a large block on a quilt's left-hand side, its visual impact may be lowered by placing several small, visually prominent blocks together in an area on the right side. When designing, try not to place large objects too close to the side edges of your quilt or too close to the middle. A big shape can also be made less conspicuous if it can be balanced by a smaller, more intricate shape. This happens because our eyes are always more interested in a complex-looking item than an object showing no change in texture, color, or value.

Jane Kakaley has created an intriguing design using the pattern Pinwheel. She has given this simple pattern added interest by changing the sizes of the blocks (photo 100B). *Plaid Pinwheels* holds interest and causes our eyes to want to study further. Her color and fabric choices have accentuated the quilt's intrigue. (See Sources for this pattern.) In *Starry, Starry Night*, Lorraine DeLaO has created a unique quilt by changing the size of her Mexican Star blocks. With her echo quilting lines, Lorraine has camouflaged quite cleverly where the blocks join one another (photo 101B).

Two Blocks Sharing the Same Background

For further block play, consider moving one block's background into its neighboring block's background. This allows the blocks to share background space. In Figure 5-8A two background corners of a Nine-Patch Star block are eliminated. When this happens the stars shift positions (Figure 5-8B). Placed in a quilt setting, a new design develops (Figure 5-8C). A similar setting is shown in Figure 5-8D, where additional squares are added as fillers to the background. This allows a feeling of airiness to prevail. Christine Porter has very cleverly eliminated most of her background area in *California Dreaming* (photo 101C). She has developed her design through shifting hues and values, causing spatial illusions.

FIGURE 5-8A

To create additional interest, move one block into another block's background by eliminating duplicate pattern pieces. This results in blocks sharing the same background space.

FIGURE 5-8B

By taking out block corner pieces, one block can move into another, thus changing the design subtly.

FIGURE 5-8C

By sharing block backgrounds, simple patterns can create innovative designs, as shown here with the Nine-Patch Star.

FIGURE 5-8D

In this setting some Nine-Patch Star blocks are sharing backgrounds while extra square fillers have been added to other background areas. Doing this allows more room for the blocks to play visually. The usual isolated pattern's static effect is either diminished or eliminated.

In Figure 5-9 the neighboring blocks share corner squares. In addition, extra background areas are created to give a feeling of openness. Filler squares are used for this purpose. Sharing backgrounds can be an effective way to create innovative designs. Construction can be done using a combination of whole and partial blocks, or you may choose to ignore the block construction by sewing pattern pieces together in rows.

FIGURE 5-9

In this setting, blocks share common background areas. Corner squares are shared with two blocks. These blocks appear to be floating, because more filler squares are added to the background.

Moving One Block's Pattern into Another Block

When using identical blocks, consider overlapping one block's foreground pattern into another block (Figure 5-10). Rearrange the pattern pieces so each block shares space with another. In the process, some foreground and background pattern pieces from the underneath block will be eliminated. Some pattern pieces may also be broken apart by this overlapping. Overlapping block patterns is more challenging than most other block manipulation methods and will require more drafting. However, the design possibilities are both exciting and limitless. A block's unique features and your own personal design style will determine the choices you make with this type of block play.

FIGURE 5-10

An exciting design can be created with a simple pattern by overlapping one block's pattern onto another block's pattern and background. Such an example is shown here.

Using value contrasts and subtle color changes when overlapping blocks may create transparency. Kathy Cosgrove created *Lucky Stars* by overlapping Nine-Patch Stars (photo 100A). Her foreground stars are made from one fabric. However, the overlapped stars (underneath stars) change in hue and value and fade into the background.

When you work with overlapping blocks, choose a block that is not too complicated. Simple designs may be much more effective than complicated ones.

DRAFTING THE PATTERN FOR OVERLAPPING

Overlapping your blocks identically throughout the design simplifies your drafting. Begin by drafting two identical patterns: the bottom block pattern and the top pattern (overlapping block). Cut the latter block's pattern pieces apart. Place them on the bottom layer's drafted pattern precisely the way you want them to be. Glue these pieces down, carefully. Then, mark and number each pattern piece. Prepare to make templates in your usual manner, using your drafted design for your pattern guide. Remember to add seam allowances to each pattern-piece template. After you have made your templates, construction can begin.

If you have made an asymmetrically overlapping design, as shown in Figure 5-10, each block must be drafted separately. Making an asymmetrical design with overlapping pattern pieces requires significant drafting. Few, if any, blocks will be identical. To begin, draft the basic pattern in its required size. Then make two copies of this drafting for each block in your quilt. Draw by hand or use a photocopy machine that does not distort or change the design size or lines as it reproduces.

Working one block at a time, use one copy of your pattern as your block's foundation (bottom layer). Cut apart the additional pattern pieces needed for that specific block's design from the second copied pattern. Place all overlapping pattern pieces for this block on the block foundation. Glue these paper-pattern pieces in place. Then, mark and number your pattern pieces. Make the block's templates in your usual manner. Continue in this manner for each block.

It's easy to create complicated designs and draft the patterns on your computer. Before purchasing an illustrator program, determine your needs, and then research the available illustrator programs. Be a savvy buyer. Many programs exist, but their offerings vary widely. I have used both Corel Draw™ and Macromedia Freehand 5.0. They are both excellent illustrator programs. Purchase a good handbook to go along with the program you choose (*Corel Draw™ for Quilters & Fiber Artists Versions 3, 4, 5, and 6* by Jan Cabral) and take advantage of your program's tutorial, if one is offered.

Staggering the Blocks

If you enjoy the feeling of nonstructured design, staggering the blocks may be great fun. It's innovative, free-moving, and definitely intriguing. Staggering allows you to place your blocks randomly on the design surface; rigidity has been eliminated.

The Nine-Patch Star is shown here in two staggered designs (Figures 5-11 and 5-12). In the first design randomly-placed blocks float above the background with only a few touching neighboring blocks. Grid lines have been included to help you see how the blocks and background relate. To create, first draft your design. Then cut the fabrics for each block. Place these unconstructed block pieces on your design wall in a randomly pleasing setting. After you are pleased with the way the blocks are interacting with each other, begin covering the background with fillers. These may be made from block pattern pieces, squares, rectangles, or any other geometric shapes that work with the design. The blocks and background fillers use the same grid system, so the different elements fit together and work well with each other. Construct in rows, blocks, partial blocks, or a combination of these.

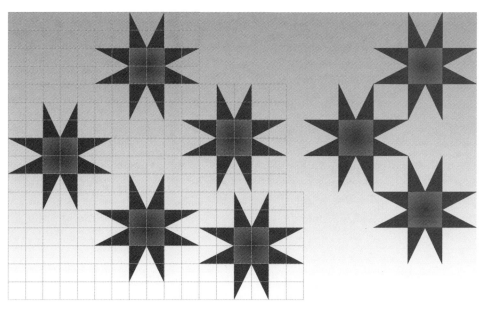

FIGURE 5-11

FIGURE 5-12

The second staggered design is shown without its grid lines. Only the stars and background are evident (Figure 5-12). In this design some blocks share background shapes. Also, a few foreground shapes overlap onto other block foreground pattern pieces. Again, the open background spaces are covered with fillers. Generally these are small squares and rectangles, although other geometric shapes may be used, too. For instance, the triangles found in the Nine-Patch Star pattern may be included in this background, if desired. If the area is large enough, a background space can be constructed from a complete block as the filler.

To get a sense of how you want to arrange your design, make several paper copies of your selected pattern. Cut them out and place them on a sheet of paper. Move the blocks around until you are pleased with the setting. You may find that you add more blocks to the fabric design; conversely, you may end up not using as many blocks as originally planned. Spaces between the blocks can be arranged in any configuration you wish— as long as they fit into the space. Once you are excited about your design, begin constructing in the area you feel most confident. This design process is similar to working on a jigsaw puzzle. The big difference is that you are actually designing the puzzle.

Floating the Blocks

It is fun to create designs where the foreground pattern appears to float above a distant background. Floating is most often combined with staggered blocks. To best create the effect of objects moving into the distance, the blocks should diminish in size as they recede into the distance. The Nine-Patch Star design seen in Figure 5-13 evokes a feeling of a starry night, with the largest stars at the bottom of the quilt and the smallest ones at the top. Here five different star sizes are used to promote this spatial effect. Because the stars change size as they recede into the distance, the fillers must change size too. The background fillers must work with the gridding system of the surrounding stars so they can be placed in the design without difficulty.

When designs are floated, the background uses more space than the foreground design. Even so, the foreground must remain dominant, if it is your focus. The colors for the background must not change the design's emphasis or upset the importance of the foreground. Avoid crowding your foreground design. It needs lots of room to float visually.

Often a floating pattern can be enhanced by color manipulation. Cool colors, grayed hues (tones), and blurred printed fabrics tend to recede, while warm colors, clear colors, and precisely-printed fabrics appear to advance. If you want to accentuate distance in your floating design, make shapes that are smaller in size, lighter in value, and more toned (grayed) in color as they move farther away. Also, the fabric designs and textures must become less pronounced and less noticeable as they become more distant. Therefore, the brightest, largest-scaled fabric prints and textures are used for areas that you want to appear closest to the viewer. Muted, ambiguous, or subtle fabric designs are used for areas that you want to appear farther away. Back sides of fabric can be very appropriate for promoting distances. By using this knowledge, along with block manipulation and background fillers, you can create dynamic floating designs.

Several quilters have used the idea of floating objects in their quilts. All are quite different from one another. The unusual and beautiful floating quilt *Utopia* has been created by Nubuko Kubota (photo 8A). It has delicate beauty and fascinating intricacy. This quilt illustrates the possibilities of blending exquisite workmanship with imagination and design play. Anita Krug's *Falling Into Place* cleverly illustrates pieces of the pattern falling away from a tightly interwoven design, resulting in a floating effect (photo 101A).

Floating designs are sensitive to visual weight, so you must be very aware of how the blocks and fabrics interact with each other. Be certain to stand back and observe your quilt as it progresses.

Shirley Kelly's *Two Minutes in May* quilt back is an excellent example of floating and staggering blocks (photo 72B). She has used innovative placement in this wonderfully imaginative design. Notice how she has balanced her design.

Carol Webb has added fillers around all blocks in *Autumn Praise* (photo 81A). This action has opened up the leaf design, making it appear as if the leaves are floating downward. Her beautiful selection of background and leaf fabrics evokes vibrancy. Another unique floating quilt design has been created by Lorraine De Lao (photo 101B).

PLANNING THE QUILT

To design a floating quilt, draw the proposed quilt's outer edges to scale on paper. If you are not certain about your quilt's size, consider using the Golden Mean ratio.

The ratio of the Golden Mean is approximately 8:13 (8 parts to 13 parts). Using this ratio, a picture that is 8 feet wide will be 13 feet long. For our use, this ratio can be converted to 1:1.625 (13 divided by 8 = 1.625). This ratio is slightly more than a 2:3 ratio.

If you know how wide you want your art to be, multiply this proposed width by 1.625. This product will be the most appropriate proportional length for your picture's width. If you want your art to be 36" wide, multiply 36 x 1.625 to find the length. In this example, the length would be approximately 58".

If however, you were certain of your artwork's length, and you needed to know the most appropriate width, divide the proposed length by 1.625 to obtain the most proportional width. For example, if you wanted your quilt to be 48" long, divide 1.625 into 48. The quotient is 29½". Thus, a quilt with a length of 48" would have a width of approximately 29".

FIGURE 5-13

Floating designs can create spectacular results with color and design play. Different-sized blocks will require extra drafting. Also, much of the surface will be broken into background fillers. These fillers can be created from a combination of geometric shapes, such as squares, rectangles, and whole blocks colored in background hues.

After the quilt's size has been determined, cut up small squares of paper or fabric in a variety of sizes. These squares represent the foreground block pattern. Arrange them throughout the surface. This design play is used to estimate spacing, location, and approximate sizes of the floating foreground. It is not meant to be an exact duplication of the actual quilt.

Once you determine how many blocks you need for your foreground design, and their approximate sizes, begin drafting the various blocks. Once these are drafted and positioned, begin planning your background fillers. Keep the background grid lines the same as the adjacent blocks' grid. To construct, think of your quilt as a puzzle. You may construct in rows, segments, partial blocks, whole blocks, or a combination of these units. Avoid getting yourself boxed into a corner. For ease, work in straight lines. There is no one right way to sew your blocks together. Many options exist.

SUMMARY

Each concept presented in this chapter should give you a wide variety of options, as well as beautiful, innovative quilts. One pattern may be enhanced by working through one idea, while another pattern may work better with a completely different treatment. There is no one right idea or way to work. While working, you may find the design evolves differently than you thought it would. There may be possibilities to create additional interest if you arrange the blocks in another way. Spontaneous change is part of the creative process. Enjoy its intervention. Have fun exploring and playing with the designs and all the available options.

Activities and Extended Learning

1. Plan a project using the idea of dropping blocks. Select a pattern that will be enhanced by this design activity. Draw a two- or three-inch paper pattern. Make twenty to twenty-five copies of the block. Play with the different ways your block can be dropped. Remember you can drop the block in a consistent manner throughout the design or you can vary the drop from row to row. For even more variety, you may even try to use fillers between some blocks.

2. Using Maple Leaf, or another asymmetrical pattern of your choice, create an innovative quilt by rotating the block throughout the design. Allow for spontaneity. Do not feel you need to finalize the design prior to beginning construction. Have a general idea of what you want to create. If you want to include any additional effects such as depth, luster, or luminosity, have an idea how you are going to work these into your design. If you want to know more about these illusions and others, read *The Magical Effects of Color* (see Sources). Think about increasing the feeling of a free-flowing design by placing fillers randomly throughout the design between blocks. Gather all fabrics that may possibly have a place in your design. Begin construction, using fabrics randomly to create each block. Play with the block placement while you construct.

3. Plan a quilt in which neighboring blocks share some of the same background shapes. Select a block that has a large enough background to allow for this interaction. Create a paper pattern; make twenty to twenty-five paper copies (two to three inches). Use these paper blocks to create an overlapping design. Consider adding fillers to your design, if you feel they will give your design more flexibility. When you are happy with your design, glue it in place on a background paper. Once the design is tentatively planned and the size has been determined, draft your pattern. Make the needed templates. Select your fabrics. Begin construction. Because the blocks are sharing shapes, it may be easier to construct your design in rows rather than blocks.

4. Choose to create a quilt using one of the following concepts: moving one block's pattern into another block; varying the blocks' sizes; staggering blocks; or floating blocks. Determine what pattern will work best with your project. Make paper blocks so you can see your design's potential clearly. Once you have determined your favorite block placement, glue the paper blocks down on paper. Determine your quilt's size.

    For any of these projects you will be dealing with multiple draftings. Work in the manner that best suits your personality and creativity. You may choose to draft each block, choose its fabrics, cut the pattern pieces, and then construct the blocks, one at a time. For some quilters, this method of working is too restrictive for creative spontaneity. If you feel this way, do not construct your quilt block by block. Instead, use the block's shapes as a vehicle to move color, value, and texture to create your design. Begin working on your design in the area you feel most comfortable. After you have placed many shapes on the design surface, you may choose to begin construction. However, you may also wait to construct after all fabric shapes have been placed on the wall. This latter method allows for great flexibility and last minute changes.

    While cutting fabrics and placing block shapes on your design wall, try to work through the design concepts as you go. Maintain unity through repetition, but also include contrast or variation. Choose your focus carefully. Also, stand back to assess your quilt's progress constantly. Visual balance will be extremely important. Do not hesitate to make changes as you work. It is difficult to assess your needs before work begins. Once the design evolves, you will begin making spontaneous decisions.

100B. *Plaid Pinwheels*, 1994, 33" x 41"

Jane Kakaley, Bellevue, Washington

This non-traditional Pinwheel quilt was created with several block-size changes, as well as innovative color and value changes. A totally unexpected design results from Jane's contemporary flair. (To purchase this pattern, see Sources.) Photo: Ken Wagner

100C. *Tribute to Tippi Hedren*, 1984, 54" x 64"

Janice Ohlson Richards, Vaughn, Washington

Janice began designing this quilt by making random lines in an empty module. After much line play, the drawings appeared to look like flying birds. Thus, this bird quilt was created. Each block uses the same line drawings, but the fabrics are changed. In addition, the block is rotated and set in different positions. The swirling quilting lines create the effect of birds flying in the wind. Photo: Ken Wagner

100A. *Lucky Stars*, 1994, 53" x 43"

Kathy Cosgrove, St. Thomas, Virgin Islands

This Nine-Patch Star pattern quilt used innovative block placement to overlap stars, which resulted in transparency. Some stars are floating above other stars, causing a design with movement, depth, and added interest. Pattern design inspired by Joen Wolfrom's presentation of innovative concepts. Photo: Alain Brin

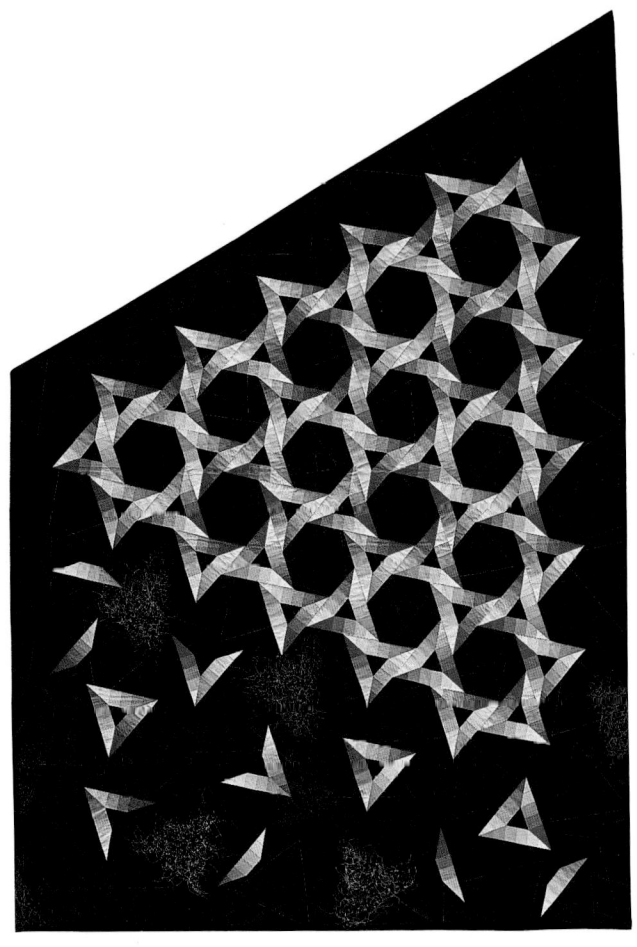

101C. *California Dreaming*, 1994, 62" x 62"

Christine Porter, Bristol, England

Christine created this quilt from fabrics she bought on her first trip to California. She wanted to create a feeling of light going diagonally through the quilt's center, with the border ranging from light to dark. This pattern comes from Camille Remme's *Starburst Mosaic*.

Photo: Neil Porter

101A. *Falling Into Place*, 1993, 60" x 86"

Pieced and quilted by Anita Krug, West Lafayette, Indiana

Designed by Cory Krug, West Lafayette, Indiana

This design was a collaboration between Anita and her son Cory. He created the basic design elements on graph paper and then challenged Anita to create a quilt from it. Anita loves the dimension that 60-degree angles create, so she was inspired to figure out how to piece the design. Triangles were assembled and stitched to hexagons. Surface embellishment, hand embroidery, and random decorative machine stitching was used. Photo: Ken Wagner

101B. *Starry, Starry Night*, 1994, 35" x 53"

Lorraine De LaO, formerly from Brentwood, California

Lorraine used the Mexican Star pattern to create her nighttime floating design. Her blocks vary in size, enhancing depth. She constructed the quilt by hand and machine, using both pieced and appliqué techniques. Her quilting lines add interest while also accentuating the stars' unusual design placement. We shall miss Lorraine's creative energy and innovative quilts. Photo: Courtesy of Lorraine's son and daughter, Christian and Victoria DeLaO

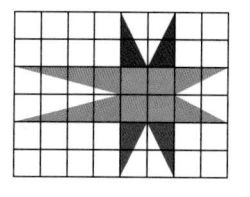

FIGURE 6-1

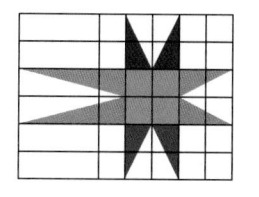

FIGURE 6-2A

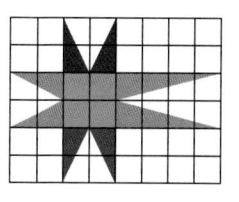

FIGURE 6-2B

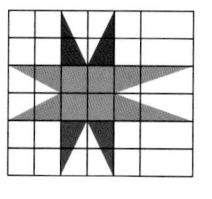

FIGURE 6-3A

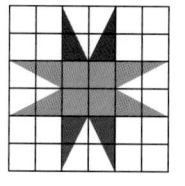

FIGURE 6-3B

Stretching the Block

Using any patch pattern, such as the Nine-Patch Star (Figure 6-1), you can create wildly exciting designs by either adding more grid lines or increasing the width between one or more grid lines in a block pattern's gridding system. For instance, to stretch the Nine-Patch Star's star points on the left side, the distance

between the first set of grid lines can be increased (Figure 6-2A). You can choose any amount of width increase. Another way to stretch the same star points would be to add extra grid lines to that side of the block, as seen in Figure 6-2B. Here two extra grid lines have been added.

To stretch the star points on the block's right side, either the grid distance can be increased, as in Figure 6-3A, or more grid lines can be added (Figure 6-3B). The same change could be made for the top star points by using either stretching method (Figures 6-4A and B). Like-wise, bottom star points may be stretched by increasing the space between grid lines or adding more grid lines (Figure 6-5). More than one block side can be stretched in any given direction. Just change the gridding wherever you wish to have stretched pattern pieces. In Figure 6-6 the lower and upper star points are both stretched.

Your block or groups of blocks can be treated much like an elastic band, bubble gum, or shrink art. With an easy change of the grid lines you can create fascinating block play by allowing each block to stretch or squeeze itself. The overall effect can evoke unbelievable illusions. The options are limitless; the designs are exciting. Enjoy working with block patterns that so willingly contort into magnificent quilt designs.

CHAPTER SIX

Fascinating Block Contortions— Stretching and Squeezing

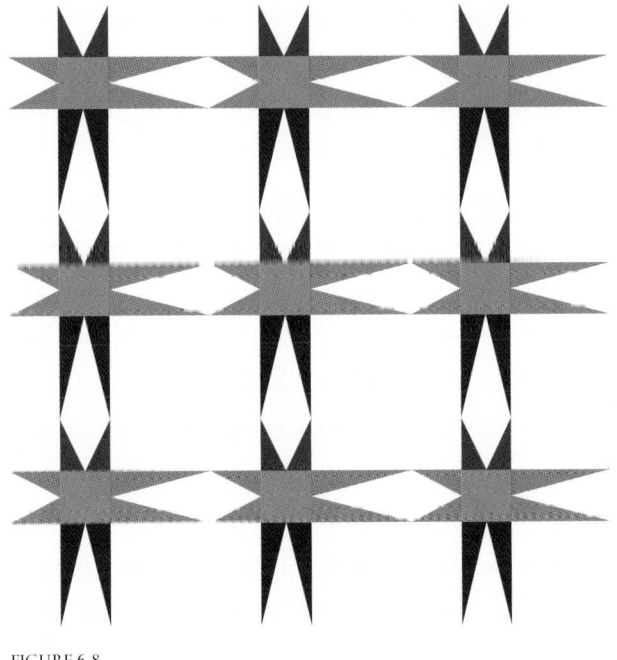

FIGURE 6-7

In this design, the star points on the block's right side are stretched. All blocks are identical. When the star points touch from one block to another, vertical diamonds and horizontal kite shapes are formed.

FIGURE 6-8

Two sides of each block are stretched in this design. When the star points touch from one block to another, inner kite shapes are formed. The background is spacious.

In Figure 6-7 the star design has been changed so all star points on the block's right side are stretched. The blocks are identical. It makes an interesting design, particularly with the kite and diamond shapes appearing in the design. In Figure 6-8 the blocks are also identical. However, stars have been stretched on the bottom and right sides. With this version the design is more open, as the background space has been stretched farther, too.

A variety of designs can be created by stretching block patterns. Even one-shape designs can be quite dynamic when stretched. Margaret Miller, master at creating fantastic designs through block-grid manipulation, proves this with *Gaslamp Quarter* (photo 82B). The triangles create striking movement as they subtly change their size.

Stretching blocks can be simple or unbelievably complex. You can make your challenge as difficult as you want. For instance, Judy White created a great challenge for herself with *Revelation* (photo 113B). This fascinating design was created with two different blocks. These were stretched to create wonderful three-dimensionality.

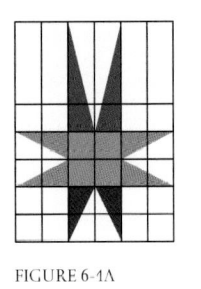

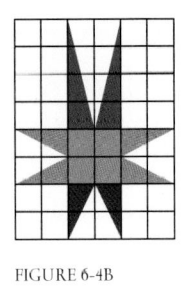

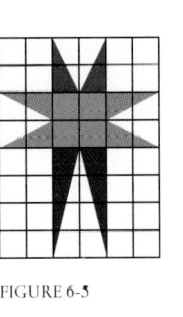

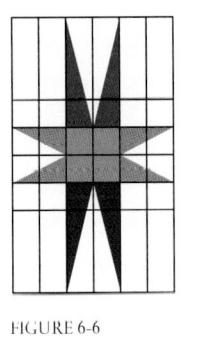

FIGURE 6-4A   FIGURE 6-4B   FIGURE 6-5   FIGURE 6-6

Stretching and Staggering the Block

If you like a more spontaneously free design, consider staggering your design while it's being stretched. Both concepts enhance each other. The staggered and stretched Nine-Patch Star is shown in Figure 6-9. To do this, make up a variety of different star blocks, using as many different combinations of stretches as you wish. Include the basic block too, if you want. Then place these blocks together in an interesting design. If possible, work from a design wall or flannel pinned to a wall. This gives you better perspective. After you have arranged your collection of blocks into a design, make fillers for the background space. Again, these fillers can be made from blocks, partial blocks, squares, rectangles, or any geometric combinations found in the design.

FIGURE 6-9

If you like a spontaneous, free-flowing design, consider both stretching and staggering the blocks, as has been done with these stars.

Analyze your overall design prior to construction to determine the easiest sewing method. You may sew the blocks together and add the fillers as you construct. However, it is very possible you will have to sew the design in a combination of rows, blocks, and partial blocks. At first glance the construction process may look overwhelming. If you break it down into manageable small steps, it will be fun.

Condensing the Block

Block sections can also be condensed, or shortened. This makes the design look squeezed. This effect is created by either eliminating grid lines or shortening the distance between two grid lines—the opposite of stretching. Thus, the Nine-Patch Star can be squeezed into a shorter version by having fewer grid lines (Figure 6-10). The top star points are half their normal length because the top grid section has been eliminated. Figure 6-11 also has shortened top star points. These were created by shortening the distance between the upper grid lines. Examples of condensed stars are shown in Figures 6-12A, B, and C. When multiple blocks of shortened star points are put together, subtle changes take place (Figure 6-13). *Eternity,* by Diana Voyer, is an excellent example of a design using condensing (photo 114A).

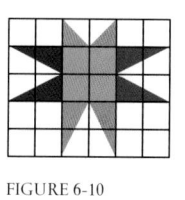

FIGURE 6-10

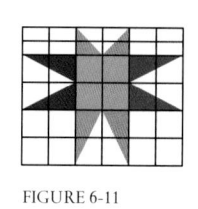

FIGURE 6-11

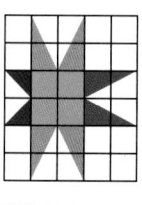

FIGURE 6-12A

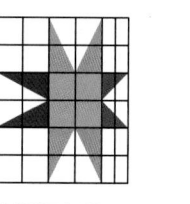

FIGURE 6-12B

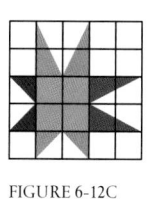

FIGURE 6-12C

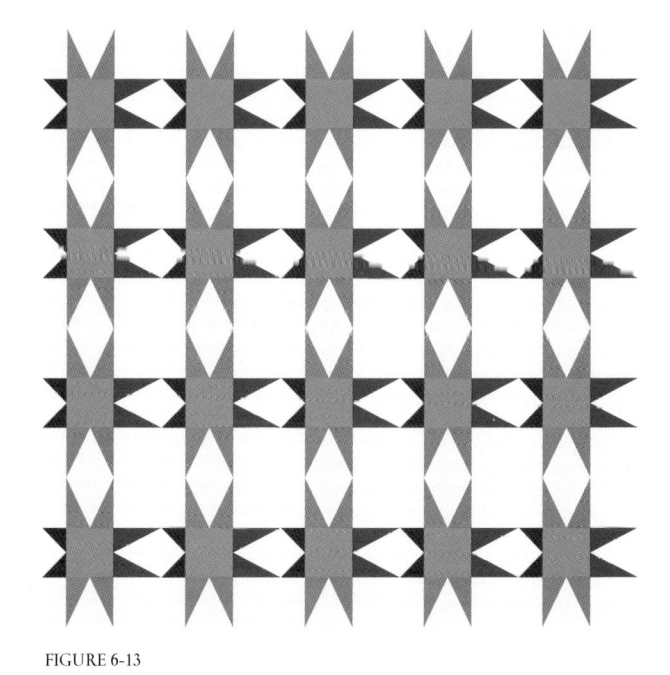

FIGURE 6-13

Your options are almost endless when creating designs with condensed areas. This is an example of a very simple, repetitive condensed design.

Rhythms of the Night (photo 113A), a beautiful quilt illustrating stretching, staggering, condensing, and floating, is created by Wendy Richardson, a talented quiltmaker who has been exploring many different types of block manipulation in the last few years. Another interesting quilt by Wendy is *Star Check: The Quilted Generation* (photo 82A) Jayne Willoughby Scott's *How I Wonder What You Are* incorporates a spectrum of ideas: stretching, condensing, staggering, and floating (photo 114B). Notice how Jayne uses her fillers to create a background that will promote her starry night.

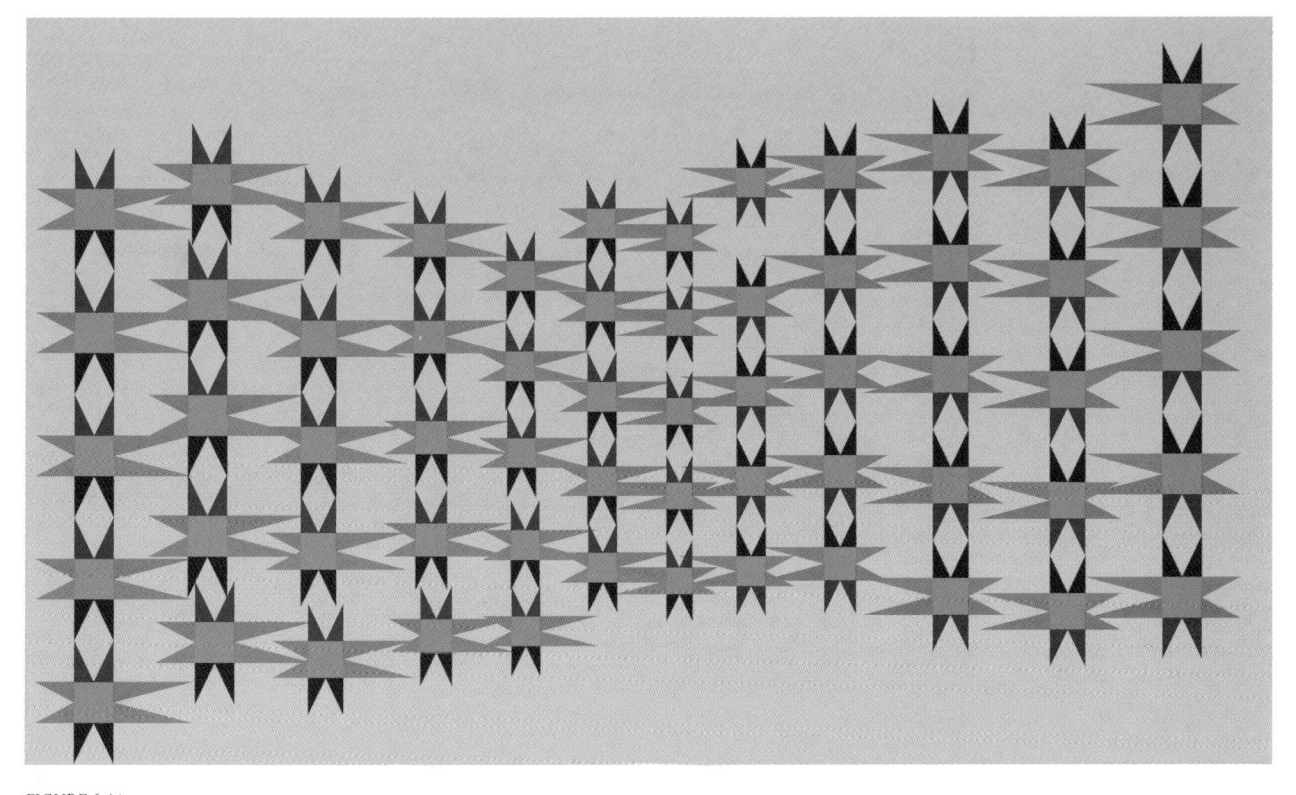

FIGURE 6-14

In this design, not only do the blocks change size as they move across the design surface, but parts of the blocks have been elongated. This adds additional intrigue to a very simple pattern. Also, the rows are dropped randomly, allowing for more flexibility.

Enlarging and Diminishing the Blocks

To give another interesting perspective, consider creating a design where the blocks continue to change size as they move across the surface design. Sometimes the blocks will be enlarged, while at other times they diminish in size. Use your imagination when arranging the blocks into a quilt design. The blocks can be traditionally set; they can be dropped; placed on-point; staggered; or floated. By changing the blocks' sizes as they move across the quilt top, horizontally, vertically, or diagonally in rows, you can create a wide variety of exciting designs.

Slight changes create subtle design play. Possibilities are shown in the following examples. In Figure 6-14 the largest blocks are positioned at the outer edges. As the vertical star rows move toward the center of the quilt, the star blocks become smaller. This creates the illusion of the center row stars being the farthest away. Notice in this design how some star points have been stretched. In addition, some blocks share their background areas with others. Figures 6-15 and 6-16 give another illusion, with the smallest blocks on each end of the quilt design. The block sizes increase, row by row, as they move toward the quilts' centers.

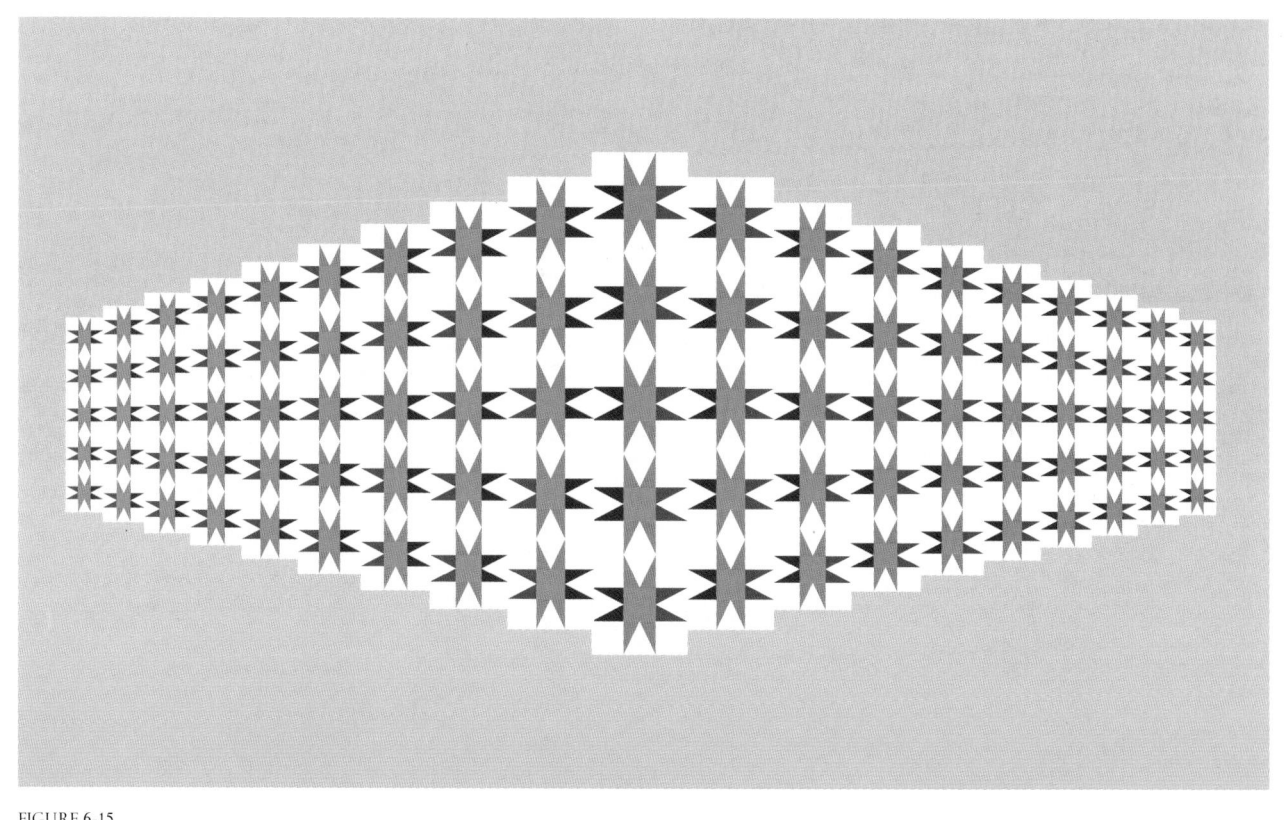

FIGURE 6-15

Interesting designs can be created when blocks are enlarged and diminished as they move across the quilt's surface. With the largest blocks in the center and the smallest ones on either side, depth can been easily achieved. Block rows have also been dropped in this example.

FIGURE 6-16

The design in Figure 6-17 incorporates changing block shapes. Most blocks have been stretched or squeezed internally before being placed in their respective rows. This combination creates several illusions. Some parts of the design appear close, while others seem to fold or move into the distance. Diana Voyer has created a quilt with similar characteristics. She has stretched and condensed her block internally, while she has enlarged and diminished her whole blocks as they are in rows. Her quilt *Eternity* (photo 114A) was inspired by Margaret Miller's work.

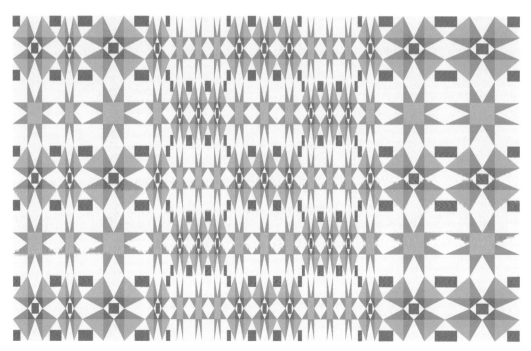

FIGURE 6-17

Inspirational Sources

Many quiltmakers have been playing innovatively with block manipulation since the early 1980s. They have created fantastic quilts through their explorations of simple changes in grid lines that cause distortions of the block pattern. In 1985 English quiltmaker Michele Walker published *Quiltmaking in Patchwork & Appliqué* (see Sources). Her book included examples of stretching and condensing blocks. More recently in the United States, Margaret Miller, quiltmaker and teacher, has been creating a wide variety of exciting illusionary quilts through grid-line changes. Her book *Blockbuster Quilts* is a welcome resource if you would like to explore further (see Sources). One of her exciting dimensional quilts can be seen in photo 82B. Alison Goss is another widely known quiltmaker and teacher who has experimented for several years with making simple block designs into dynamic quilts. Some of her original inspirations have come from Acuma Indian designs. Her quilts flow like music. See *Ancient Directions* on page 61 in *The Magical Effects of Color.*

Many people shy away from stretching or condensing block patterns because these designs look so intimidating at first glance. However, the drafting is relatively easy, although it may be time-consuming. Almost all designs created in this manner are visually stimulating. If you enjoy drafting, love visual challenges, and need a new project, contorting blocks is a fascinating avenue to investigate. Have fun!

Activities and Extended Learning

1. *Stretching Blocks*

   Choose a simple block pattern from which to experiment with the stretching-block concept. Draw a small paper pattern of the design. Make certain the grid lines are apparent. This can be a simple line drawing, or you can color it, as has been done in Card Tricks in Figure 6-18A. Next, draw the perimeter lines of another block (the same size), but only draw the grid lines that would be used for your selected pattern. In this example, Card Tricks can be drafted with three equal divisions horizontally and vertically, so the block needs only two grid lines in each direction to make these separations (Figure 6-18B). After you have drawn both blocks, make several copies of each for your design play. Then it's time to play.

   Take one patterned block and cut away one side (Figure 6-18C). This side will be the one that will be stretched. Next, take a gridded block and cut out as many gridded sections as you want placed on your patterned block. In Figure 6-18D two gridded sections have been used from a gridded block, but you could use a different amount. You could place the entire gridded block of three divisions on your block's cut-away side. You could even add four or more sections, if you wanted a very elongated design. To do so you would have to use more than one block for your gridded sections. After you have replaced the patterned block's cut-away space with the grid rows, redraw that block's left-side pattern (e.g., Figure 6-18E). If you are working in color, color these newly stretched pattern pieces. Your first stretched block should be complete (Figure 6-18E). Then create another elongated block, using as many sections from your gridded blocks as is necessary to create the amount of stretch you desire. Remember you can stretch the pattern in any direction. You can also stretch more than one side. Once you have done several, begin placing them in an overall design. Play with your blocks until you are pleased with their setting. Include fillers if your design appears to require them.

You may want greater flexibility in stretching than your gridded blocks give you. If that is the case, you can simply draw your own gridding system with whatever stretching you wish to incorporate. In Figure 6-18F the two right vertical rows are identical to the pattern block's grid. However, the left grid section has been stretched without regard to any particular measurement. This can be done simply by drawing the new stretched section on another piece of paper and gluing it to the pattern block. In Figure 6-18G the left-hand vertical grid row has been created in the same manner, but it is a bit narrower than the elongated grid section in Figure 6-18F. After the newly drawn gridded section is attached to a pattern block, the new pattern lines can be drawn. Again, they may be colored if you wish (e.g., Figure 6-18H). Drawing your own grid line distances allows your design to stretch into any space you wish. You can reconfigure your blocks using both methods, if you want.

Experiment with your design so you are aware of how the pattern looks when it is stretched in different settings. If you enjoy the way your pattern reacts to grid stretching, begin designing a wall-size quilt. Start in the area that seems most comfortable for you to begin. You might decide to take one block and create an elongated grid to use for the central focal design (Figure 6-18I) After you have worked out your grid, draw your design. Use the grid lines and intersecting points as your references to draw the pattern (Figure 6-18J). After you have created one section, begin playing with the rest of the design. If your started in the center, begin working outward. You can make an extremely elaborate design, or you can create a very simple design as seen in Figure 6-18K.

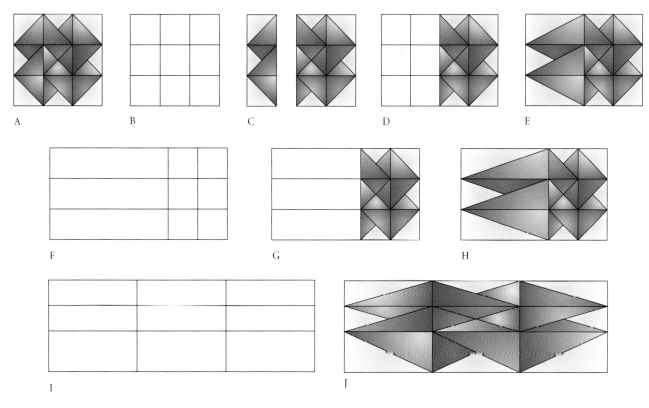

A   B   C   D   E

F   G   H

I   J

FIGURE 6-18A–J

FIGURE 6-18K

2. *Condensing the Block Pattern*

Select a simple pattern to play with block condensing. A symmetrical pattern (a balanced block with identical quadrants or halves) is easier to work with than an asymmetrical design (one which does not have identical components). The asymmetrical pattern Maple Leaf was used for this example (Figure 6-19A). The same concepts apply whether you use a symmetrical or asymmetrical block.

FIGURE 6-19A

If you want to work very simply with the condensing concept, begin by make a paper drawing of your pattern. Be certain to include the grid (e.g., Figure 6-19B). You may leave your pattern block as a line drawing, as shown in Figure 6-19B, or you can color it. Now make another square the same size as the original block. Draw twice as many grid lines in this square as was needed to draft your selected pattern block (e.g., Figure 6-19C). Then make several copies of the gridded and patterned blocks.

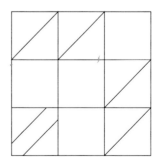

FIGURE 6-19B

Determine which pattern part you wish condensed in your pattern block. Then cut away that gridded section from the block (e.g., Figure 6-19D). Next, cut the width you want to use from your gridded block and place it on your patterned block (e.g., Figure 6-19E). Then draw the design, using the new grid. The pattern will have a squished look on one side (e.g., Figure 6-19F). Remember, you can condense more than one side of your block pattern if you wish (e.g., Figure 6-19G).

If you want even greater flexibility in condensing your design, begin by drawing twice as many grid lines in both the pattern block and the block grid. Thus in Maple Leaf, the pattern block would have six divisions horizontally and vertically (Figure 6-19H). Then it is quite easy to take out any of the block's inner grid sections. Simply cut away the unwanted section and bring the remaining parts together as shown in Figure 6-19I.

3. *Combining Stretching and Condensing Block Patterns*
To create more flexibility in your design, consider combining stretching and condensing in your selected block. This will allow great illusions to appear in your design. In Figure 6-20 the Maple Leaf has been both condensed and stretched. This is only one of many possibilities. Some sections can be greatly exaggerated while others are diminished.

4. *Enlarging and Diminishing the Design*
Create a design that includes changing the blocks' row sizes. This will result in a feeling of perspective, promoting the effects of folding, curving, and perhaps moving rows. You may use only one block pattern, or you may want to create a design combining two different patterns, such as seen in Figure 6-17 (page 107). After you have determined your quilt's size, and the size of your selected block(s), figure out each row's block width. Have fun creating movement and three-dimensionality with your block rows. You may choose to draft all blocks before you begin construction, or you may draft the pattern as you work.

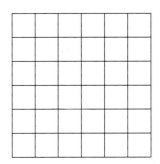

FIGURE 6-19C

FIGURE 6-19D

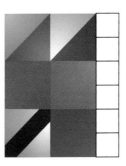

FIGURE 6-19E

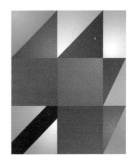

FIGURE 6-19F

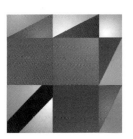

FIGURE 6-19G

FIGURE 6-19H

FIGURE 6-19I

FIGURE 6-20

5. *Create a Design By Stretching and Condensing the Quilt's Blocks*
Select one pattern to use to create a design with stretched and condensed blocks. The pattern Century of Progress can be an exciting design to use (Figure 6-21A). Next, determine your quilt's proposed dimensions. Then divide the quilt's design surface into a variety of rectangles and squares. These should vary in size. You can create amazing designs by changing the block sizes while you stretch and condense these patterns. One design possibility using Century of Progress block is shown in Figure 6-21B.

Either draft your blocks as you construct, or draft everything prior to construction. Select the fabrics you plan to use. Begin constructing your quilt wherever you feel most comfortable. These designs can be quite exciting to create. Enjoy every stage: selecting the block, planning the quilt, selecting the fabric, drafting the blocks, constructing, and quilting to add enhanced texture.

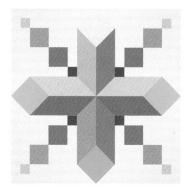

FIGURE 6-21A

FIGURE 6-21B

113A. *Rhythms of the Night*, 1991, 80" x 96"
Wendy Richardson, Brooklyn Park, Minnesota

Wendy created this quilt to illustrate the feelings she has about the connection between flowers and stars, and heavens and gardens. Besides being emotionally appealing, *Rhythms of the Night* has additional visual excitement because of the way Wendy chose to manipulate the pattern grid. The stars appear to stretch out as they twinkle in the sky. Photo: Ken Wagner

113B. *Revelation,* 1990, 52" x 48"
Judy White, Ellington, Connecticut

Judy began this quilt by placing a star on a cube. Then she manipulated the design until it formed a pattern she liked. The stretched design, along with the fabric and color choices, creates wonderful illusions of depth, transparency, and luminosity. Photo: Ken Wagner

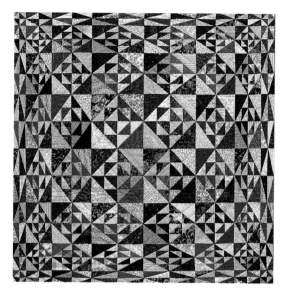

114A. *Eternity*, 1993, 51" x 51"

Diana Voyer, Victoria, British Columbia, Canada

Diana has created a marvelous example of manipulating the block pattern to create an unusual design. She was intrigued by Margaret Miller's work, which was shown in *Quilt with the Best*. Using Margaret's information as a guide, Diana created *Eternity*. Photo: Ken Wagner

114B. *How I Wonder What You Are*, 1994, 58" x 80"

Jayne Willoughby Scott, Victoria, Edmonton, Alberta, Canada

Jayne created a dynamic design by combining Nine-Patch blocks with Fifty-four-Forty or Fight blocks. Note that Jane has created a quilt with varying block sizes. Jayne's goal was to create an innovative design using perfect points. She used a precision paper piecing technique shown to her by Linda McGeehee. Photo: Gail P. Hunt

CHAPTER SEVEN

Old–Time Favorites Forging New Paths

Many traditional patterns continue to be popular after generations of use. We are seeing numerous quilters use traditional patterns as a jumping-off point to their own creative adventures (photos 15B and 76A). The results are wonderful. Since we have hundreds of traditional patterns available to us, why not use some of these designs as inspirations for your own exploration or interpretation? To whet your appetite and get you into the mood, this chapter presents several quiltmakers and their innovative quilts. Perhaps you will be compelled to explore one or more of these traditional favorites in your own way. I hope the quilts presented here will start your own imaginative juices stirring so you may create a show-stopper of your own.

The Window— Changing Architecture

Window quilts have taken quite an interesting turn in the last decade. While some quilts are related to the Attic Window pattern, others are merely visual suggestions of windows. Window quilts give interesting perspectives from diverse vantage points. They are great starting points for beginning a design. Almost any scene set behind a window or framework can be a visual treat, with a little imagination. Look around at homes in your community. Find a window that inspires you. Duplicate its features and use it as a framework with which to work.

The traditional Attic Window pattern can be varied to give the quiltmaker latitude with her design (Figure 7-1A, B, and C). Linda Gill's *Windowscape* (photo 121A) is a traditional Attic Window with subtle light effects created through clever fabric placement. Martie Huston has chosen to add interest to her design by placing one window on-point within another window. This rotation adds dimension to *Butterflies in My Window* (photo 117B).

FIGURE 7-1A
Attic Window (nine-patch pattern: 3 x 3 = 9 square grid)

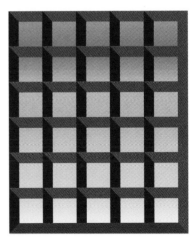

FIGURE 7-1B

Attic Window quilts are wonderfully diverse. You have many options. In this Attic Window design, the window frame repeats two colors throughout the surface, while the background colors change subtly.

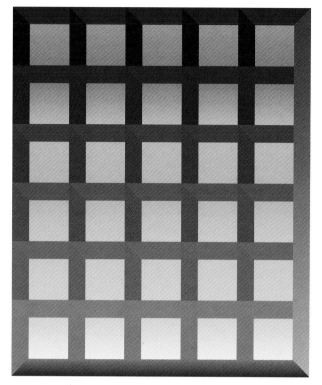

FIGURE 7-1C

In this Attic Window design, both the background and the window frame change their colors subtly. It is one of many options, which may be chosen for an Attic Window quilt.

Karen Comb's *Attic Windows: From a Different View* was inspired by Islamic designs and patterns. She challenged herself by placing simple traditional block patterns inside each window frame (photo 117A). Karen had to draft her pattern in perspective in order to create this ingenious optical illusion. As hinted by the title, this view is seen from a different perspective than in other window quilts.

Anita Krug's *Something Fishy* has a much more open feeling than most Attic Window quilts, because she has eliminated some window framing (photo 117C). This is an interesting visual design variation. Anita created light effects by changing the window frame's hues and values. In *The Best Time of Day* the silhouetted frame enhances the beautiful sky and garden view beyond. Here, Anita has created a calming picture (photo 121C).

Caryl Bryer Fallert's *Autumn Perspective* is wonderfully complex and very different from the others (photo 83B). Her background scene, intricately pieced from

vertically-placed fabric strips, weaves in and out of view with stunning effect. Caryl wanted to create a three-dimensional window setting with an abstract landscape behind it. Since the autumn colors are her personal favorites, she chose an autumn landscape. She drew all the windows full size, using one-point perspective. After drawing the windows, she drew the landscape. Caryl wanted to create the feeling of looking out at a forest in autumn, without actually being able to identify any one object. This she has done quite successfully. Some windows are quilted in leaf patterns. The brown window frame is quilted in a wood grain pattern.

Caryl's *Through the Gazebo Window* is an unbelievable, breath-taking quilt (photo 71A). Again, Caryl has intricately broken up her landscape to create her picture. Caryl's goal was to create a landscape with a very literal, three-dimensional foreground, which faded into a more abstract background. This landscape became a composite of her favorite springtime images. The working drawing was full-size. Using more than three hundred different fabrics for her color palette, Caryl strip pieced fabrics together to create the scene beyond. Caryl worked intensively on the scene for three months. Then she spent an additional two months hand quilting it. If you see *Through the Gazebo Window* in an exhibit, you will find this a most delightful, extraordinary view. (See Sources for ordering information for Caryl's book *Caryl Bryer Fallert: A Spectrum of Quilts, 1983-1995.*)

In my own window quilt, *Dreaming of a Room of My Own*, I too wanted a fairly realistic view (photo 121B). One of my goals was to blend my favorite techniques into one quilt. I used traditional piecing for the wallpaper, hand appliqué for the window frames, representational strip-piecing for the distant landscape, and vertical impressionistic strip-piecing for the wisteria and garden plants growing downward and upward at the window. For ease, I created the landscape in two different sections: the lower window and the upper window. The window's horizontal cross bar visually and technically connected the two window sections together after each was completed. Once the scene was strip-pieced, I hand appliquéd the windows onto the design. After straightening the scene, the wallpaper triangles were sewn together and applied to the design.

117A. *Attic Windows: From a Different View*, 1994, 47" x 53"
Karen Combs, Columbia, Tennessee

This innovative Attic Window quilt was inspired by Islamic designs and patterns. Its skewed design is quite effective. Photo: Courtesy of the artist

117B. *Butterflies at My Window*, 1991, 50" x 50"
Martie Huston, Santee, California

Butterflies at My Window is another example of the enormous diversity of one particular block pattern, Attic Window. Here it appears the viewer is looking down at the window. The background fabric was covered with butterflies; hence the name. Quilted by Joyce Baromich. Photo: Ken Wagner

117C. *Something Fishy*, 1989, 49" x 64"
Anita Krug, West Lafayette, Indiana

After taking a class from Judy Mathieson, Anita was excited to create a 60-degree angle window quilt. She drafted the design using three values of peach and turquoise fabrics for the window; fish fabric was bought for the background. Because Anita wants the viewer to focus on the center of the quilt, she subtly arranged the color values to achieve this intent. Photo: Ken Wagner

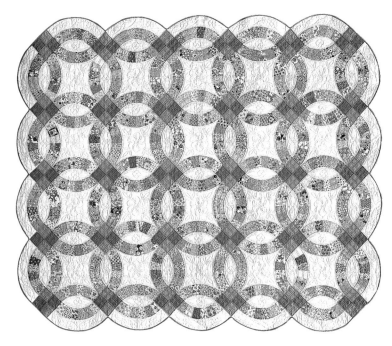

118A. *Double Wedding Ring*, 1930-31, 93" x 78"
Pieced by Minnie V. Shinn, Kansas City, Missouri
Quilted by Genevieve S. MacDuff, Fox Island, Washington

This quilt exemplifies the beauty and nostalgia of the historic Double Wedding Ring pattern used by so many quilters in the past. Mrs. Shinn pieced this quilt; later her daughter, Mrs. MacDuff, quilted it. It is now lovingly cared for by its proud owners Jack (son of Genevieve MacDuff) and Harriet MacDuff. Photo: Ken Wagner

118B. *Double Wedding Ring*, 1995, 86" x 86"
Arlene Stamper, San Diego, California

Inspired by Mary Schafer's vine border, shown in *Sets & Borders*, Arlene drafted a Double Wedding Ring quilt, creating a border using her own appliquéd tulips and leaves pattern. The sawtooth border, inspired by Jeanna Kimball's quilt *Hexagon Rose Wreath*, was created by piecing all the triangles on the machine. Arlene used a "float" set so the edges would be straight, not curved. She used her own method for sewing the rings together. Photo: Ken Wagner

Unbroken Circles—
The Double Wedding Ring

Double Wedding Ring quilts have long been a favorite for many quilters. Generations of newlyweds have received these beautiful quilts to celebrate their new marriage. One lovely historic Double Wedding Ring quilt is shown in photo 118A. It was pieced by Minnie Shinn and quilted by her daughter Genevieve MacDuff. The date on this quilt is 1930. It is now owned by her son and daughter-in-law Jack and Harriet MacDuff. Arlene Stamper has created a lovely Double Wedding Ring quilt with a floating setting (photo 118B). Her gray and apricot rings are accentuated by a delicate floral border. Arlene's design has been beautifully enhanced by her hand quilting. This quilt, although made in contemporary times, still has a nostalgic taste of history.

Two modern-day interpretations of the Double Wedding Ring pattern are done by Grania McElligott and Junko Sawada (13B and 40B). *Fractured Rings* uses silk fabrics to develop a beautiful rich design. As is characteristic of a great many non-American quilts, Grania's design and fabric selection create all of the textural effects; there are no quilting stitches. *Sazanami* is soft and subtle in its presentation. This quilt was inspired by the hydrangeas and June's rainy season in Japan. Junko pictured the mirrored image of hydrangeas metamorphosed into colorful water rings by sudden raindrops. The variation of lightness and brightness has a stereoscopic effect on the image of repeated water rings. Azure or purple flowers are reflected in a pool of water under a gray sky. The offset placement of the rings creates a contrast within the soft endless circles.

Each of these examples is quite different, representing history, charm, beauty, modern sophistication, and imagination. As we can see, the design gives varied opportunities to play with colors and fabrics. Because simplified construction versions of this pattern are available, you have the option to create designs using an intricate historic pattern or one of modern simplicity.

Successful Samplers

Traditionally, sampler quilts are created from a combination of block patterns. These can be pieced, appliquéd, or a blend of both. Most traditional sampler quilts appear to have twelve to twenty-four different blocks. Although many beginning students make sampler quilts as their first project, it is actually one of the most difficult styles of quilts to make beautiful or visually successful.

A sampler quilt's visual balance is achieved by first selecting designs that will work well together. Each selected design must be able to enhance the others. No one block can be so powerful that it overwhelms the other blocks, unless, of course, it is featured as the primary focus block. The need for unity throughout the entire design is equally important. Therefore, a unifying factor must be apparent throughout the blocks. A visually identifiable theme is one helpful way to begin. Philomena Durcan's lovely *Celtic Clan* and Rosey Hunt's intriguing *She's All at Sea* are both theme quilts. Their theme blocks help to create a sense of unity that is so important to the visual success of sampler quilts (photos 13A and 13C).

Another unifying factor is color. Using similar colors throughout the quilt achieves a sense of unity. Repeating fabrics unifies colors. If no one fabric is used throughout, certainly repetitive coloration should be considered. In *Friendly Challenge* Peggy Hill, Barbara Godfrey, and Connie Tenpass combined the same purple and orange mottled fabric to make their three-block sampler quilt. Each quilter planned and created her own block. Although the blocks are quite different and their visual weights differ, the color use has blended the three blocks into a unified statement (photo 80B).

Visual balance is of prime importance in a sampler quilt. Each block's visual weight must be considered carefully during placement. It can be extremely difficult to place pieced blocks together so they are balanced or attract equal attention. It is more difficult to combine pieced and appliquéd blocks. Most pieced blocks are heavier than appliquéd blocks, so blending the two techniques must be done carefully. Appliquéd blocks can be equalized by increasing the intensity of a few colors (making the hues more pure) or by lowering the values of some colors. A creative way to help achieve balance is to vary the size of your sampler blocks.

Exciting Group Quilts— Sharing a Theme with Friends

Group friendship quilts have always been popular. They are great gifts for mutual friends or for special circumstances. They, too, can be difficult to create with visual success if no ground rules or clarifying thoughts have been given. Special effort should be made to unify the quilt. Sometimes this means using one or two fabrics in all blocks, or choosing a visual theme strong enough to unify the blocks. The latter was done effectively by three different quilting groups. With each, the group selected an interesting theme, set design ground rules, and then used their skills and talents to create wonderful quilts.

In 1993 The Tuesday Quilters, a group from the Washington D.C., and Maryland area, completed a most unusual friendship quilt. Their novel design idea was to challenge themselves to make a unique group picture quilt of a historic landmark. They chose Lafayette Square. A photograph of the square was divided into nine vertical sections. Each quilter was given one division. From this photographic strip each quilter was challenged to create a seven-inch by thirty-seven-inch fabric rendition of her particular picture section. Each quilter worked independently, using only the photo as her guide. They tried to remain faithful to the scale and colors in the photo. The result was the charming quilt *Lafayette Square* (photo 75A). The Tuesday Quilters members who created this quilt were Kathy Vitek, Donna Radner, Lynne Bradley, Lauren Kingsland, Verena Levine, Ann Hoenigswald, Lee Porter, Amy Frank Lindberg, and Carol Clanton.

Lafayette Square proved to be such a fun challenge that five of The Tuesday Quilters joined four other quilters to create another picture quilt of an historic site. They chose Georgetown. The selected photograph of Fletcher's Boathouse and the Georgetown skyline was cut into nine strips and distributed among the participants. Lauren Kingsland provided backing, batting, a full-sized simple line drawing of each strip for reference, and a snapshot of the whole scene. Each quilter then rendered her picture strip as she chose. She could emphasize whatever she wanted within her section. Communication between the quilters was permitted. After all panels were finished, they were assembled into the quilt *Georgetown on the Potomac* (photo 75B). Quilters who took part in this project were Kathy Vitek, Lauren Kingsland, Sarah Sagalow, Verena Levine, Lee Porter, Gertrude Braan, Carla Bonfasi, Michelle Gilchrist, and Amy Frank Lindberg.

Far from the east coast another group of quilters avidly created their own version of a group friendship picture quilt of their favorite historic site. The Ladies of the Lake from Manitowoc County, Wisconsin, challenged themselves to recreate The Rahr Mansion in quilted panels. Shirley Suettinger challenged group members to create this quilt in the spring of 1994. Although the group was apprehensive about their ability to create a quilt of the beautiful Rahr Mansion, they agreed to meet the challenge. Each quilter was given one eighth of the mansion's drawing. They were asked to reproduce their portion of the picture in a finished size of seven inches by fifty-one inches. There was no communication or viewing of each other's panels until the unveiling party. This lovely group quilt (photo 8IB) was then presented to the Rahr West Art Museum, which is attached to the back of the Rahr Mansion. The quilters who created this novel friendship quilt included Phyllis Krueger, Sally Kahlenberg, Brenda DeBruyn, Claire Amato, Judy LaGrow, Jean Lowden, Lucy Zeldenrust, and Shirley Suettinger.

121A. *Windowscape*, 1994, 43" x 58"
Linda Gill, Novato, California

Windowscape, an Attic Window design, was a value-study quilt for Linda. She used values to create depth and dimension in the window view. Not only has Linda gradually changed the values in the background scene, but she accentuated the dimension further by changing the horizontal and vertical window ledges. Photo: Ken Wagner

121B. *Dreaming of a Room of My Own*, 1991, 80" x 94"
Joen Wolfrom, Fox Island, Washington

An impressionistic view from an open window was originally begun as an Attic Window quilt. However, the more the design played in my mind, the less rigidity I wanted in my window frame. Thus, a Palladian window was substituted for the more traditional Attic Window frame. Photo: Ken Wagner

121C. *The Best Time of the Day*, 1993, 43" x 55"
Anita Krug, West Lafayette, Indiana

A white fabric with black grasses/leaves found on a flat-fold table was the genesis for this quilt by Anita. After she dye-painted over it, the fabric lines called for simple piecing. Once the main part was pieced, Anita added the arched top, creating the illusion of a window. The quilting lines follow the lines of the leaves and grasses. The machine quilting in the borders has architectural lines around the window, replicating wood molding against brick walls. Photo: Ken Wagner

Innovation Overstepping Traditions

Innovative ideas are flowing like a swift-running river in quiltmakers all over the world. It is exciting to see the novel ways quilters are looking for inspiration, designing their quilts, and creating their visions in fabric. Traditional techniques are being expanded and new methods are exploding before our very eyes. This is a very exciting time to be a quiltmaker. I hope you will consider incorporating some of your own innovative ideas in your next quilting project.

When working with new ideas you may find traditional construction methods either impossible to use or not applicable. Consider exploring new construction methods. You may use alternative techniques that have been recently developed. Or you may want to work by trial and error, developing your own innovative construction methods. You will be energized when you engage in personal exploration. Your work will have vitality.

Increase your technical skill level and your awareness of design possibilities as much as possible by taking classes, reading, and going to exhibitions. It is crucial to have a strong foundation, so you have the confidence to tackle any project that appeals to you. However, the most important step you can take to increase your own creativity is to make quilts that consistently force you to learn new skills and expand your ideas.

As you begin working innovatively, do not attempt to control your work too tightly. Allow new ideas to spawn as you work. Rigidity and creativity are not compatible partners. While working spontaneously you will be presented with many unknowns. There will be many creative risks. Your overall success may depend on your point of view. Unexpected or unplanned results are often thought of as mistakes. However, they are actually opportunities to learn, stretch, grow, and develop new techniques and ideas. Therefore, it behooves you to view "mistakes" in a positive manner rather than regard them as examples of failure. When you encounter a step that gives you great difficulty, think of it as an opportunity to challenge your brain, rather than as a problem. The steps to success have much to do with our attitude and point of view.

Give yourself ample credit for taking risks and finding ways to meet challenges. Be proud of your innovative accomplishments, as they are a unique expression of your inner self—the most priceless, remarkable gift you can give. Because your creative time is so precious, choose to spend this time creating quilts that speak from your heart instead of working on projects that have little real meaning to you.

In order to allow for growth and innovation, we all must be willing to provide a safe arena for everyone's exploration. When this happens we can feel comfortable with exploring, risking, and creating in whatever manner we choose. Challenge yourself to use a traditional pattern or style and create a uniquely individual quilt of your own.

Activities and Extended Learning

1. Begin thinking about creating an innovative window quilt. Keep your eyes open for interesting window designs. Look at homes in your neighborhood for design possibilities. Also, look through magazines, newspapers, and window manufacturing brochures. At the same time your are formulating your window ideas, visualize different possibilities for the imagery behind your window panes. This planning may take a few days, a week, a month, or even longer. Let the ideas simmer in your mind as long as you wish.

   After you have determined what you would like to do, begin drawing your design. Plan the techniques you will use. Consider using a combination of techniques, such as piecing, appliqué, and stitchery. If you will be piecing only, perhaps you will consider working with several different piecing methods.

2. Choose a traditional block with which to experiment in a design. After you have selected it, allow yourself several brainstorming sessions. During this time write down all ideas that come to your mind for your quilt. Do not make any judgments about your ideas at this stage. Accept all ideas. Don't concern yourself with technical need, skills required, or design difficulties. Allow your brain to play with lots of ideas before you come to a decision. This may take a few days, a week, a month, or more. Don't force your ideas, as your brain works best when given time to let the seed of an idea germinate in your mind.

   When you have several ideas, evaluate all of them. Choose the one that seems to present the most interesting appeal. Make a small drawing of the selected block (two to four inches). Make as many copies as you need to experiment with your design ideas. Formulate your plan. Determine how you will construct your design. Select your fabrics. Begin construction. During construction, feel free to veer from your initial plan if another idea seems to please you more.

3. With a small group of quilting friends, plan to make a group picture quilt. As a group, select the quilt's theme. Gather several photos of your selected theme, or research any available historical photos. After all photos have been gathered, have the group select one preferred photo. Make a color photocopy of this original photo. Divide the photocopy so each quilter is assigned to one section of the picture. Then reproduce the divided photocopy so each quilter has her own sample of the entire picture. Also have the picture enlarged to its proposed finished size. Divide and cut it apart. Give each person her own full-size pattern section.

   The group should determine any necessary ground rules and the tentative completion date before construction begins. It is important to decide what will be done with the finished quilt prior to beginning the project.

Taking a Creative Leap— Planting a Seed; Watching It Grow

It is impossible to go to a quilt show without seeing many contemporary quilts, which incidentally were either rare or nonexistent prior to the 1980s. The number of contemporary quilts expands each year. It is exciting to watch this creative growth take place. Many quiltmakers have made important contributions to the world of contemporary quilt art. Leading quilt artists in the world include Dorle Stern-Straeter, Caryl Bryer Fallert, Deirdre Amsden, Margaret Miller, Erika Odemer, and Janice Richards. Some of their beautiful quilts can be seen in photos 16B, 71A, 78A, B, and C, 79A and B, 82B, 83B, 86A, 100C, 125A and B, 133B. Their art quilts vary in technique and style, but all are exquisite in design and technical application. Each of these persons has influenced quiltmakers throughout the world with her magnificent work. If you are fortunate enough to be able to attend one of their classes or see quilts made by Dorle, Caryl, Deirdre, Margaret, Erika, or Janice, do so. It will be a rewarding experience.

Other innovative contemporary quiltmakers whose work can be enjoyed in this book include Emilie Belak, Jean Liittschwager, Joy Baaklini, Reynola Pakusich, Judy House, Sylvia Einstein, and Laura Heine. Their work can be seen in photos 15A, 16A, 42B, 70B, 77A, 84B and C, 85A, 126A and B, 129A, B, and C, 130C, and 133A. We are fortunate because our field is filled with talented people from all parts of the world. Their creative energy has spawned unbelievable art in almost every possible style. With our field's exploding diversity, it is apparent everyone is capable of spawning her own creative growth, if she wishes to do so. No one person or group of people owns the world's creativity. Each of us has the capability to create unique and beautiful quilts once we are in tune with our own individual style. Admittedly, it takes courage to take those first steps. Initially, most of us are petrified we may fail. This fear of failure keeps many people away from experimenting on their own. Dare to ignore these fears. Take the chance to believe in yourself and your creative potential. Once we assuage our fears, we find there is great joy in risking and working towards creative goals. Once infected by the creative bug, it is impossible to stop the ideas from coming forth. Our energy level rises, and we amaze ourselves with both our creative ability and the level of our accomplishments.

Taking the First Step

Perhaps you would like to stretch your imagination further by making your own designs. Start slowly if this is a new idea for you. Use a block pattern, a specific shape, a group of shapes, or an idea as a jumping-off point to create your own design. Several quilts illustrate the great versatility in using blocks or specific shapes as a creative foundation for the quiltmakers' own original designs. Examples include *Reef* (photo 7A), *Utopia* (photo 8A), *Sunlight and Winds* (photo 9A), *Starlit Night* (photo 16B), *Oblique Illusion* (photo 41A), *Adam's Outer Realm* (photo 41C), *Kaye-oss* (photo 73B), *Gaslamp Quarter* (photo 82B), *Building Memories* (photo 83A), *Introspection* (photo 84A), *Falling Into Place* (photo 101A), and *Deep Sea* (photo 125B). Most assuredly, there is no one right

125A. *Flying Free #1*, 1993, 22" x 22"
Caryl Bryer Fallert, Oswego, Illinois

Flying has always represented freedom to Caryl. *Flying Free #1* was the beginning of a series of quilts exploring the idea of the flight of one's imagination. A variation of the traditional Flying Geese block was incorporated into one of the curved and tapered templates. The free-form machine quilting was done without marking. Caryl, an internationally renown quilt artist shares her work and ideas in her new book *Caryl Bryer Fallert: A Spectrum of Quilts, 1983-1995* (see Sources). Photo: Courtesy of the artist

125B. *Deep Sea,* 1993, 75" x 55"
Dorle Stern-Straeter, München, Germany

Using a kite-shaped block, Dorle used color and value contrasts to create the rich, beautiful *Deep Sea* quilt. In this design the blocks are tessellated and the pattern is mirrored. Photo: Patricia Fliegauf

126A. *I See the Moon,* 1991, 57" x 64"
Joy Baaklini, Austin, Texas

This quilt depicts many levels of personal and spiritual symbolism displayed as images of past, present, and future in the mind of the daydreamer. Intentionally, the puppet has no strings attached. While making this quilt Joy did not consciously see it as a self-portrait, but now she feels it speaks for all women who dream of things past, present, and future. Joy was inspired by the desire to make an art quilt, and the puppet's body was the beginning seed of this intriguing quilt. Owned by: Sharron Banks. Photo: Carina Woolrich. Courtesy of Quilt San Diego

126B. *The Dream,* 1996, 55" x 62"
Joy Baaklini, Austin, Texas

Musing over the profound experience of creativity and self-expression, Joy symbolically answers her own question about creativity in *The Dream.* Joy feels her naive approach is most apparent in the relaxing of the anatomical figure and the mischievous, playful quality of the tree. The creative spirit in the tree teases the dreamer to let her imagination fly free. A cryptic epitaph of painted symbols alludes to a journey of self-discovery. The symbolism and creative spirit exhibited in *The Dream* are wonderful.

way to work, as creative thought is so uniquely individual. Begin with an idea and work as spontaneously as possible. When venturing into this world of original design, you do not need to meet anyone's expectations or standards. It is important to enjoy your experience while you gain insights, knowledge, and skills. During this period of exploration, do as your spirit moves you. Your design may be only a small step away from a traditional quilt pattern, a blend of a traditional block and other design inspirations, or perhaps an avant garde design with no traditional influences (photos 12A, 14A, 15B, 16C, 41D, 70A, 77B, 81A, 113B, 130A and B).

Choose ideas that excite you. Do not feel you must stay within the confines of a block design if other ideas capture your interest. There are many options available to you. Determine which ideas you are most drawn to. Then include these in your next project. You may wish to work with a representational design as seen in *In Praise of Poppies* (photo 85A), *View from My Childhood Garden* (photo 10B), and *Dreaming of a Room of My Own* (photo 121B). You may wish to create a visual story such as *Two Minutes in May* (photos 72A and B), *The Last Panda* (photo 15C), *I See the Moon* (photo 126A), or *The Dream* (photo 126B). Or you may want to play with the idea of combining blocks or block parts with representational images. Examples of these types of innovative designs include: *Sunlight and Winds* (photo 9A), *Bethany Beach* (photo 14B), *Canada Geese Metamorphosis* (photo 15A), *Transition* (photo 16A), *Through the Gazebo Window* (photo 71A), *Autumn Perspective* (photo 83B), *Tribute to Tippi Hedren* (photo 100C), *Rhythms of the Night* (photo 113A), and *Old Growth* (photo 133A).

New concepts come to us in many forms. For instance, the actual idea for *Canada Geese Metamorphosis* (photo 15A) came from the relationship of the traditional block Flying Geese and flocks of Canada geese flying over British Columbia on the way south and north. While camping one summer, Emilie Belak's ideas began to evolve. She created a silk-screen print in 1982. As a math teacher with a special interest in geometry, Emilie likes the work of M.C. Escher. She decided to unify all with the use of Escher's idea of metamorphosis. Emilie was limited by the width of sky fabric, since she didn't want a seam in

the sky. She overdyed the gray sky fabric with light blue. She also tried to be more creative with the border by incorporating both kinds of "geese." There are three rounded corners and one right-angled one.

Allow your creative juices to explore further once you determine the path you wish to take. You do not need to know everything about your design before you begin. You may feel comfortable about one portion of your design, but you may not be able to visualize the entire quilt. If you wait for all to be crystal clear, you may never start. Begin where you are most comfortable in the design. Miraculously, as you proceed, your subconscious mind quietly processes design ideas for the unclear areas. Then, by the time you reach the area of uncertainty, everything has fallen into place.

Sometimes you may find you have boxed yourself into a corner while working on a design. Or perhaps it seems to be fighting you. If it appears you cannot get a handle on your design, give yourself permission to end the project. Set a time to stop your design play. Then sew the quilt together when the time limit has been reached. Set the work aside. At a later time you will be able to look at it and discern one or more possible paths you could have taken.

I took this course of action several times during my early years of creative experimentation. Often my frustration level rose because I couldn't put into fabric what I saw in my mind. Sometimes it was because my ideas were too ambitious; sometimes it was because I didn't have a clear enough idea of what I wanted to do. At other times I had trouble simply because I lacked design understanding. When I found myself hopelessly lost, it was time to cut my losses, learn from my project, and start again on a fresh slate. Although these projects weren't visually successful, I learned a lot from them. Each helped my creative growth—even if I didn't think so at the time. I have found the creative process of each piece I have made was an opportunity to further my creative growth. In the end, the visual results were not nearly as important as the learning involved. Every project cannot be expected to be a superlative design experience, but personal creative growth can be assured.

Creating Your Own Design Style

You develop your own style when you give yourself enough time to explore. People recognize your artwork because it has a certain uniqueness to it. You will soon find your own visual cadence. For instance, Laura Heine's two quilts *I Valued My Plaids* and *Best of Both Worlds* (photos 129A and B) are dissimilar in design, yet carry a strong family resemblance. Thus, it does not surprise us to learn these are created by the same person. Deirdre Amsden's quilts illustrate her own style very well (photos 78A, B, and C). Her design style has evolved through many years of creative adventure. Dorle Stern-Straeter's quilts also have a familiar creative thread. She has developed her own style by working through her creative ideas (photos 16B, 79A and B, and 125B).

To create an original design, be familiar with the various design elements and principles. This does not mean you must work rigidly within a formula. However, you should know the design parameters and determine what your focus will be. Your quilt should not be a haphazard display of fabrics without rhyme or reason. To begin a new design, ask yourself a few basic questions. These could include such questions as: What is your intention or goal? How will you achieve the focus? Will you accentuate through line, color, value changes, directional changes, scale, or proportion? What shapes or pattern will you use to carry out your ideas?

Once you clarify your ideas about the roles of the design elements, give some thought to how you will arrange these into a visual composition. How will you achieve unity throughout your design? Generally, unity can be achieved through repetition, proximity, or gradation. Repetition or gradation often evoke movement and rhythm. This, then, brings about harmony and unity. Don't forget that too much unity results in monotony and disinterest. So if your design is quite repetitious, make certain it contains a point of contrast or variation to create further interest.

Begin with an easy design goal and work slowly toward more complex design challenges. If you make your design assignment too difficult, you will frustrate your-self. This results in procrastination, total defeat, or a disastrous design. As a guideline, give yourself only one major challenge for each project. As you work, you may want to abandon your course because new ideas have evolved. Rely on your intuition to tell you what is best to do. Savor the time you have given yourself for creative exploration. It feeds the creative soul.

Be certain to stand back and observe your quilt as it progresses. An original design's success depends heavily on balance and visual weight. Use a design wall (e.g. flannel or batting pinned to a wall or board), so you can watch your design develop. Stand back frequently to see how it is progressing. Fabric art is similar to an oil painting. Standing too close gives an inaccurate view of the total picture.

TAKING IMPORTANT DESIGN BREAKS

Take breaks as you work. Your mind needs a rest from focusing on the quilt's design and the challenges you have given yourself. Walk away from your work to give your mind time to clear itself and begin relaxing. Another very important reason for taking a break is to allow your subconscious mind to create new trains of thought. This innovative thinking happens after your brain has been introduced to a challenge. While your conscious mind is resting, your subconscious (right brain) mind will begin finding new ways to work through design problems. Your brain loves this challenge. It will work overtime for you even though you may not be aware of it. It is especially active while you are sleeping or engaged in daily chores.

During this design break an occasional fleeting thought will pass through your conscious mind while you are doing other activities. This fleeting idea, or vision, is your subconscious mind relaying a message to you. Do not discount or ignore this idea. Quite possibly it will be the clue to unlocking any design dilemmas you have. Also, it may be an innovative thought, introducing you to a new or unexpected design path. No matter what you are doing or where you are, take the time to write down these fleeting thoughts. They are truly keys to

129B. *Best of Both Worlds*, 1991, 39½" x 70½"
Laura Heine, Billings, Montana

Laura created her own design using an original block pattern as her starting point. With innovative color choices she has created an exciting quilt. Notice the similarities in design and color between Laura's two quilts (129A and B). Even though both quilts are quite different, one can tell the two are works by the same person. Laura has developed her own pronounced style by encouraging herself to develop her own ideas. Photo: Ken Wagner

129A. *I Valued My Plaids*, 1992, 57½" x 71"
Laura Heine, Billings, Montana

Laura has used the quadrilateral triangle, a one-patch design, as the foundation for her color and design play. The result is a fascinating design using a multitude of plaids. Again, the similarities and differences are quite striking between this quilt and *Best of Both Worlds* (129B). Photo: Ken Wagner

129C. *Tamaki's Legacy*, 1994, 64" x 49"
Judy House, Alexandria, Virginia

The inspiration for this quilt came from a garden photo Judy had taken. The resulting design is a loose interpretation of the garden. Using the concepts of Ikebana, the art of Japanese flower arranging, the basic design format is that of a triangle. *Tamaki's Legacy* was named in memory of Judy's Ikebana teacher. Photo: Courtesy of the artist

130A. *Sunrise in Winter,* 1984, 30" x 24"
Joen Wolfrom, Fox Island, Washington

Sunrise in Winter, an example of a "strip-pieced puzzle" design, was created from fabric strips of varying widths and lengths rather than from strip panels or modules. The design surface was broken into many divisions much like a straight-lined jigsaw puzzle. The intrigue was in figuring out both the color play and the puzzling construction sequence. Photo: Ken Wagner

130B. *Fortissimo in Plum,* 1985, 60" x 36"
Joen Wolfrom, Fox Island, Washington

The curved design in *Fortissimo in Plum* illustrates the illusions of luminosity, depth, and transparency. The author used the curves-on-the-whole technique which she devised in the early 1980s for use in many of her curved-design commissioned works. For further discussion about this quilt style and technique see page 134.
Photo: Ken Wagner

130C. *Lutry,* 1983, 46" x 46"
Sylvia Einstein, Belmont, Massachusetts

Sylvia used the traditional pattern Jacob's Ladder as her design foundation for creating this original design. In addition, the design was inspired by the medieval town Lutry, nestled on the shores of Lake Geneva, where Sylvia once lived. For further discussion about this quilt, see page 131. Photo: Courtesy of the quilt artist

your personal design style. After returning from your break, look over your notes and study your design. Your intuitive self will quickly analyze your progress and determine whether you should continue on your previous path or move in another direction. Again, work as intuitively as possible.

Abstract Block Designs

When you first begin working on original designs, follow a sequential learning pattern. If you have always worked with block designs, don't give up the comfort zone of this format with your first creative experiences. Instead, find ways to use the block while exploring contemporary design. Most of our renown innovative quiltmakers began in this manner. Two contemporary quilt artists who used the block format to begin their creative exploration are Sylvia Einstein and Janice Richards.

In one of Sylvia's early original designs (*Lutry*, photo 130C), she began with the traditional pattern Jacob's Ladder. Sylvia first drew the Jacob's Ladder pattern on graph paper. With pencil and eraser, she began changing lines and shapes. As she worked, the well recognized Jacob's Ladder pattern slowly disappeared. The design began to remind Sylvia of the tiny medieval town of Lutry, Switzerland where she once lived. The nostalgic scene of vineyards, Lake Geneva, and palm trees fluttering in the warm breeze tightly surrounding the town of Lutry continued to play in her mind. Eventually a dynamic design evolved with a sense of the nestled town's reflection reverberating off the shore of Lake Geneva. The contrast of confined, tightly spaced shapes surrounded by vibrating waves of openness have been beautifully created to represent the relationship between the town and its surrounding environment. Combining a block design with an intuitive or nostalgic idea from the past, as Sylvia has done, can create a wonderfully innovative design that is personally satisfying.

Janice Richards also began her first contemporary exploration within the block format (*Tribute to Tippi Hedren*, photo 100C). She drew many lines and erased a lot before she eventually created a block pattern she liked. Janice made copies of her block and then began placing the blocks in different arrangements. As she played, birds seemed to appear in the design. This idea excited her, and thus her quilt's design began to unfold. She figured her block and quilt dimensions, drafted the block, and made pattern templates.

Janice pinned cotton batting to her wall for a temporary design wall. She proceeded to cut fabrics from her templates and placed them on the batting in their respective block spaces. She began by using solid-colored fabrics. Then she found a decorator fabric with slashes of color that worked perfectly to simulate light hitting the birds as though they were in motion. The bird design began to develop quickly. Janice wanted to evoke the feeling of sunrise to sunset. However, when she used one fabric for each background pattern piece, it was not as visually appealing as she had envisioned. Therefore, she changed her course by making strip-pieced fabric panels for her sky. When she replaced her sky fabric with this new fabric, her quilt suddenly came alive. Highlights and shadows appeared. As Janice's design progressed to her satisfaction, she began constructing the blocks. When all blocks were completed, she sewed the blocks together. To accentuate the birds in flight, Janice quilted their lines of movement.

Many of us began our strip-piecing experience with Log Cabin, Seminole, Lone Star, and Trip Around the World designs in the late 1970s or early 1980s. Because beautiful fabric was scarce then, it often became necessary to create our own fabric to meet our needs. The easiest way to do this was to use either the crazy-quilt or strip-piecing method. When it became apparent that luster, highlights, shadows, and depth could be attained by manipulating strips of fabric, contemporary quilters began using strip-piecing as an avenue for creative exploration. Now strip-piecing is used regularly in both traditional and contemporary quilts. It is highly popular because of its diversity. Making your own strip-pieced fabric allows you to combine different fabrics into a more interesting presentation than if you use only one fabric. It is particularly useful when you want subtle value changes or a lustrous effect. Combining strips which contain value and color changes can produce almost limitless design possibilities.

I learned a great deal about color interaction when I made color and value studies with contemporary strip-pieced designs in the early and mid 1980s. Each month I gave myself an assignment to create a small wall quilt. Often these were created using strip-pieced fabrics. These projects gave me the opportunity to experiment with design, color, and value manipulation. Although I made unbelievable mistakes in both design and color application while creating many of these small strip-pieced quilts, now I have a solid understanding of color and design as a result of these activities.

Currently, many people are experimenting with strip-pieced designs. Strip-pieced contemporary designs are very popular now. Innovative use of strip-pieced techniques include quilts in photos 15C, 71A, 83B, 86A, 121B, 125A, 126A. Sylvia Einstein enjoys combining strip-piecing and geometric shapes in her original designs. *Lutry* is one such example (photo 130C). Many moods and effects can be achieved through strip-piecing. For instance, Erika Odemer's *January Quilt* vibrates with power and intrigue with her strips of strong colors and diagonal direction (photo 86A) while *View from My Childhood Garden* promotes quiet gentleness with its soft colors and horizontal direction (photo 10B).

During my 1980s strip-piecing exploration, I enjoyed making *strip-pieced puzzle* quilts. These designs were created from strips of varying widths and lengths rather than from strip panels or modules. The design surface was broken into many divisions, much like a straight-lined jigsaw puzzle. The fun was in figuring out both the color play and the puzzling construction sequence. This design play is very intuitive. An example of a strip-pieced puzzle quilt is *Sunrise in Winter* (photo 130A).

Using Geometric Shapes

After you have had some experience, you may wish to move out of the confines of the block. For your first experience, consider working with only one shape. Use a shape you enjoy working with to convey your visual imagery. Again, determine your design goals, your focus or direction, and what elements and principles you will use to accomplish these. Your imagination can offer you unlimited design ideas when working with shapes.

Some of the most beautiful contemporary quilts use primarily one type of shape. Judy Breytenbach's beautiful *Reef,* using a wide assortment of triangles, is rich with color and design movement (photo 7A). This quilt is breathtaking as you stand before it. Judy House mainly uses triangles to create her abstract quilts (photo 129C). Her training in Ikebana (Japanese flower arranging) and her design instincts help to create Judy's pronounced style.

Reynola Pakusich's *Circles II and Circles III* are beautiful contemporary quilts, using circles as the repetitive design shape (photos 84B and C). Each area of these quilts is filled with fabric and color intrigue. Again, they are intuitively created.

133A. *Old Growth*, 1990, 56" x 33½"
Jean Liittschwager, Leaburg, Oregon

The background of *Old Growth* is made from
simple triangles and blocks influenced by the
power and simplicity of the Amish Sunlight
and Shadow and Wild Goose Chase patterns.
These background blocks are enhanced by
the use of shimmering silk, rayon, polyester,
and metallic threads to create the impression
of sunlight filtering through the trees to the
forest floor. Photo: Courtesy of the artist

133B. *September Falls*, 1988, 52" x 70"
Janice Ohlson Richards, Vaughn, Washington

An impressionistic picture of salmon
jumping a waterfall on the way to their
wilderness spawning ground was created by
using several different block modules. These
modules were designed so they could be
broken apart and easily combined with other
module units. Fabric and color placement
were important elements in creating this
abstract design. Photo: Ken Wagner

Curves-on-the-Whole: Free-Flowing Curves

I am particularly fond of curved designs. I love their gentle, soft, free-flowing spirit. I began experimenting with these designs in the early '80s because my heart and mind yearned for more free-flowing designs than the traditional geometric shapes could give me. My first designs were fairly structured, as I used a compass with extensions. However, I soon found perfect circles and semi-circles were too constraining for my personality. I began drawing my designs free-hand on large paper. This scared me at first, because I never considered myself artistic. As I gained experience, I relaxed and my drawings improved. Because these curves extend themselves throughout the whole design surface, I named them *curves-on-the-whole* to differentiate free-flowing curves (photo 130B) from curved block patterns such as Double Wedding Ring.

Over the years it has been fun seeing others experiment with this design style. Organic curves are often soft and calming. Rosemarie Guttler creates elegantly sophisticated free-flowing designs with unbelievable skill (*The Visual Dance,* page 29). Naturally, curved designs do not have to be demure. They can be exciting. Caryl Bryer Fallert's *Flying Free #1* promotes drama rather than quietness (photo 125A). Curves are particularly wonderful for organic-style designs and realistic interpretations, such as Emilie Belak's *In Praise of Poppies* (photo 85A). Quilts using curved designs may be extraordinarily diverse, because they often draw on intuitive design sense. Several techniques can be used to create these quilts. Currently, many quilters are experimenting with this organic design. Within the next decade the number of free-flowing curved quilts will multiply immensely. This will be a fascinating genre to watch as the designs unfold further in diversity and intuition.

SUMMARY—"BREAKING RULES" TO CREATE YOUR IDEAS

If you have a design idea you wish to pursue, use the most appropriate method to attain the effect you want. Do not feel confined to traditional techniques or rules if these methods do not allow you to create your desired effect. Do what your heart and mind see and feel. In that way your work becomes individually yours.

Breaking boundaries or rules is a time-honored tradition in all art. For instance, the Impressionists were originally shunned because they did not paint the proper subject matter or use the correct painting techniques of their time period. With few exceptions, their work was not accepted into the prestigious shows of their time. The Impressionists struggled in their creative endeavors because they believed in their right to create from their souls. Eventually their work was no longer ostracized or viewed as outrageous. It became the popular style. Now these painters and their work are revered throughout the world. Since their emergence many other styles have evolved. So it is with all art, including quiltmaking. All traditions were once innovative ideas in the spectrum of ever-changing creative thought.

We should be careful not to be judgmental when viewing a quilt that does not agree with our visions or with "acceptable" methods. In order to allow for growth and innovation, we must be willing to provide a safe arena for everyone's exploration. Quality innovation begets a new genre; eventually it becomes part of the broad spectrum of accepted traditions. Enjoy bringing innovative changes to traditional favorites, if this is your desire. Be excited about trying new ideas; do not apologize to yourself or others for your experimentation.

Activities and Extended Learning

1. Plan an abstract design (suggesting a scene or other representational idea) using a block pattern. Select a block that will be used as the vehicle for your picture quilt. Draw a scaled design of your proposed quilt, or draw your quilt's design full size. Make a design wall with flannel, batting, or other material before beginning your quilt. Draft your pattern; make the templates. Select your fabrics. Begin laying out the fabric pieces on your design wall. Once you have a section of your quilt laid out, you may put those pieces together. Construct by rows or blocks. To view scenic quilts using blocks or portions of blocks, study quilts made by Janice Richards (photos 100C and 133B), Jean Liittschwager (photo 133A and 16A), Beth Gilbert (photo 14B), and Sue Atlas (photo 42A).

2. Choose your favorite geometric shape. Plan a quilt using this shape. Determine what your intention or goal will be. What will be your design's focus? Will you accentuate your design through line, color, value changes, or directional changes? How will you achieve unity throughout your design? After you have formulated your ideas, lay out your design on paper. Draft your pattern, if appropriate. Make any templates you need. Select your fabrics. Begin constructing your quilt where you feel most comfortable.

3. Allow yourself to play in your next design project. Create the quilt you have dreamt about or have seen in your mind. Proceed in small steps. Give yourself permission to risk. Relax. Remember this is not your last quilt. It is simply one step along the way in your quiltmaking—a means of self-expression. Never conscientiously attempt to make your "masterpiece" while experimenting. Since perfection and creativity are not mutually compatable, this goal puts too much stress on your creative endeavors. Most of all, have fun. Enjoy yourself. That should be the primary reason for you to create quilts.

Patchwork Block Pattern Play

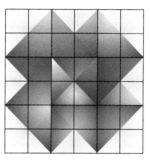

Card Tricks (nine-patch pattern:
6 x 6 = 36 square grid)

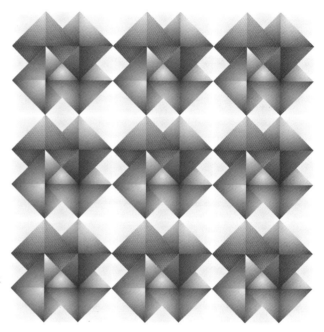

Card Tricks traditional block
setting (nine blocks)

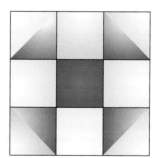

Shoofly (nine-patch pattern:
3 x 3 = 9 square grid)

Shoofly traditional block setting
(nine blocks)

Century of Progress
traditional block set
ting (20 blocks)

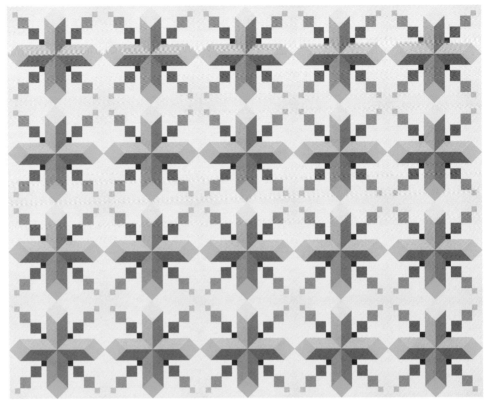

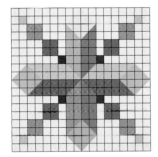

Century of Progress (nine-patch
pattern: 18 x 18 = 296 square grid)

Century of Progress ad-
ditional block play—
dropping block rows

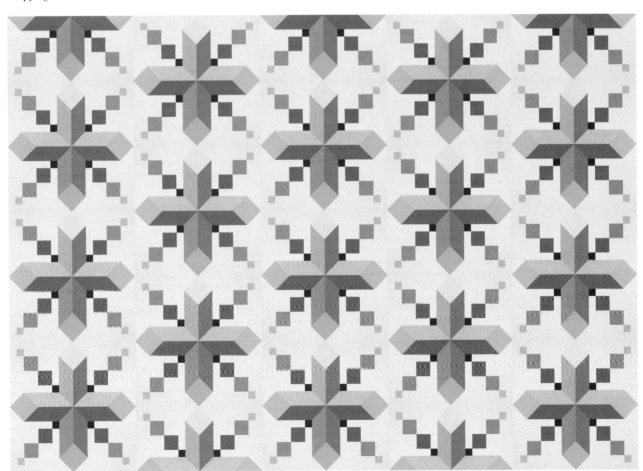

Road to Oklahoma traditional
block setting (nine blocks)

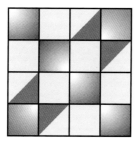

Road to Oklahoma (four-
patch pattern: 4 x 4 = 16
square grid)

Road to Oklahoma additional
block play—rotating blocks

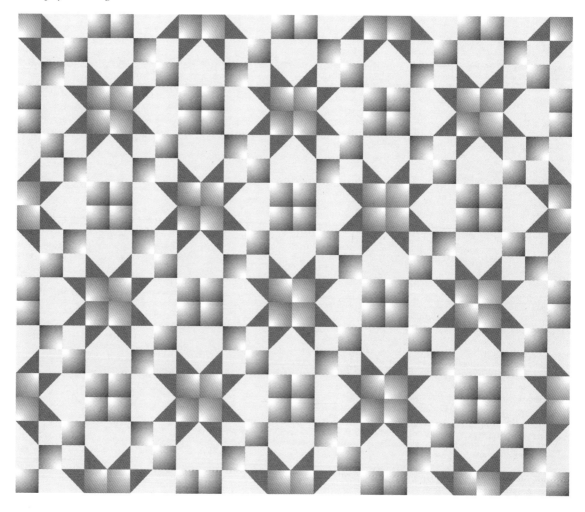

Double X, No. 3 traditional
block setting (nine blocks)

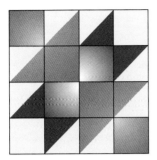

Double X, No. 3 (four-patch pattern: 4 x 4 = 16 square grid)

Double X, No. 3 additional block play—
rotating blocks one-quarter turn

1904 Star additional block play—
alternating block coloring

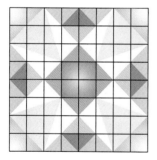

1904 Star (four-patch pattern:
8 x 8 = 64 square grid)

Index

Photo pages appear in **bold face** type.

Sources

OTHER BOOKS BY JOEN WOLFROM:

Joen Wolfrom has written three previous classic, best-selling books. If you would like to include these books in your resource library, either request them at your local quilt store or contact C&T Publishing at P.O. Box 1456, Lafayette, California, 94549, USA (telephone: 1–800–284–1114).

The Visual Dance: Creating Spectacular Quilts by Joen Wolfrom (1995): Explore, experiment, and solve the mysteries of design in a simple, positive way, so that you create quilts and wall art with confidence and excitement. This book includes a wealth of ideas, design basics, and other essential information which will make each quilt you create dance with visual beauty and interest. It is an excellent resource and is highly recommended by many of our nation's leading quilting teachers.

The Magical Effects of Color by Joen Wolfrom (1992): Using nature as her guide, Joen unlocks the mysteries of color, relating color theory to our daily observations and reactions. She discusses how to use color naturally, elaborates on nature's most beautiful color schemes, and reflects on the emotional aspects of color. Joen also describes visual illusions in detail, giving instructions for creating iridescence, luminosity, luster, shadows, mist, transparency, and highlights.

Landscapes & Illusions: Creating Scenic Imagery with Fabric by Joen Wolfrom (1990): Have you ever watched the sun go down, breathed the misty air before a storm, or been mesmerized by the newly-fallen snow, and wondered how you could capture the essence of those experiences in your quilts? Joen's first best-selling book will lead you through the planning and construction steps to create strip-pieced fabric landscapes that reflect the ever-changing moods of nature. With Joen's precise, clear information on color and fabric, you will learn how to create visual illusions such as depth, luminosity, reflection, and mist that add drama and emotion to your scenic imagery.

OTHER SUGGESTED RESOURCE BOOKS
FOR YOUR PERSONAL LIBRARY:

Appliqué 12 Easy Ways! by Elly Sienkiewicz, available from C&T
Publishing, Lafayette, CA.

Blockbender Quilts by Margaret Miller, available from Margaret at
P.O. Box 798, Woodinville, WA 98072.

Caryl Bryer Fallert: A Spectrum of Quilts, 1983-1995 by Caryl Bryer Fallert,
available from P.O. Box 945, Oswego, IL 60543, or AQS,
Paducah, KY.

A Celtic Garden, Celtic Spirals, and Celtic Quilt Designs by Philomena
Durcan, available from 834 W. Remingon Drive, Sunnyvale,
CA 94087.

Colourwash by Deirdre Amsden, available from That Patchwork Place,
Bothell, WA.

Dimensional Appliqué by Elly Sienkiewicz, available from C&T
Publishing, Lafayette, CA.

Elegant Stitches by Judith Baker Montano, available from C&T
Publishing.

Encyclopedia of Pieced Quilt Patterns compiled by Barbara Brackman,
available from AQS, Paducah, KY.

Faces & Places by Charlotte Warr Andersen, available from C&T
Publishing, Lafayette, CA.

Feathered Star Quilt by Marsha McCloskey, available from
Feathered Star Productions, 7221 3rd Ave. N.W., Seattle,
WA 98117.

Firm Foundations by Jane Hall and Dixie Haywood, available from
AQS, Paducah, KY.

Log Cabin Quilts by Bonnie Leman and Judy Martin, available from
Leman Publications,
Wheatridge, CO.

Pattern Play by Doreen Speckmann, available from C&T Publishing, Lafayette, CA.

Pieced Borders by Marsha McCloskey and Judy Martin, available
from Crosley-Griffith Publishing Co., Inc., 1321 Broad Street,
Grinnell, IA 50112.

Quiltmaking in Patchwork & Appliqué by Michele Walker, available from
Ebry Press, London.

Scrap Quilts by Judy Martin, available from Crosley-Griffith
Publishing Co., Inc., 1321 Broad Street, Grinnell, IA 50112

Small Scale Quiltmaking by Sally Collins, available from C&T
Publishing, Lafayette, CA.

Strips That Sizzle by Margaret Miller, available from Margaret at
P.O. Box 798, Woodinville, WA 98072.

FABRIC SOURCES:

Aspidistra Sequenced Hand-dyed Fabrics (great value range by
Jack Bishop)
7231 120th Street, Suite 493, Delta, B.C. V4C 6P5, Canada
e-mail: rbishop@bc.sympatico.ca

The Cotton Patch Mail Order, 3405 Hall Lane, Dept. CTB,
Lafayette, CA 94549
e-mail: cottonpa@aol.com / 800-835-4418 / 510-283-7883
A Complete Quilting Supply Store

Lunn Fabrics (lovely range of hand-dyed fabrics by Debra Lunn
and Michael Mrowka)
357 Santa Fe Drive, Denver, CO 80223.

Sky Dyes (beautiful and exquisite hand-painted fabrics by Mickey
Lawler)
83 Richmond Lane, West Hartford, CT 06117.

Spiller Dyeworks (wonderfully intense and gorgeous hand-dyed
fabrics by Tina Spiller)
2524 Pine Bluff Road, Colorado Springs, CO 80909–1316.
Send $5.00 for color card and sample packet.

PATTERNS AND ADDITIONAL TECHNICAL SOURCES:

For strip-pieced, six-pointed star instructions, purchase *Not Your
Grandmother's Stars* by Marcia Baker at Alicia's Attic, 1609 Mullins
Drive, Plano, TX 75025.

For information about pieced-picture patterns of original designs
available by Cynthia England, send LSASE to England Studios, 803
Voyager, Houston, TX 77062.

For information about her available pieced patterns, send LSASE
to Jane Kakaley, P.O. Box 1342, Bellevue, WA 98009.

For a wide selection of original appliqué patterns and instructions, write to Jeana Kimball's Foxglove Cottage, P.O. Box 18294,
Salt Lake City, UT 84118.

About the Author

Joen began quiltmaking in 1974 after she left her career in the educational field to become a homemaker. Her interest in color, design, and contemporary quilt art surfaced in the early 1980s. During that time Joen challenged herself to experiment with new techniques and visual ideas. She is noted for being the innovator of several techniques, including strip-pieced landscapes and organic curved designs (*curves-on-the-whole*). She was the innovator of the *free-form freezer paper technique*, which is often used in curved and straight-line piecing. Her work is included in collections throughout the world.

Joen has taught and lectured in the quilting field both nationally and internationally since 1984. In addition, she is frequently invited to jury and judge international, national, and regional shows. Previously published books are *Landscapes & Illusions: Creating Scenic Imagery with Fabric*, *The Magical Effects of Color*, and *The Visual Dance*.

Joen's other interests include gardening and landscape design, playing bridge, reading, and spending quiet times with friends and family. When not traveling, Joen enjoys the private quiet of her family's home in a rural setting on a small island in Washington State. There she enjoys life with her three children and husband—Danielle, Dane, David, and Dan.

Inquiries about workshop and lecture bookings and other correspondence may be sent directly to Joen Wolfrom at 104 Bon Bluff, Fox Island, Washington 98333. Requests for a current teaching schedule may be sent to the same address (include a large self-addressed, stamped envelope).

Other Fine Books from C&T Publishing

For more information write for a free catalog from
C&T Publishing, Inc.
P.O. Box 1456, Lafayette, CA 94549
(800) 284-1114
http://www.ctpub.com